LIVE WHAT YOU LOVE

LIVE WHAT YOU LOVE

The 20 Golden Secrets of Business Attitudes to Succeed

Build Your Internet Business Empire Without a Loan
Or a Premiership Footballers Salary

Jean TCHAMGUE

authorHOUSE®

AuthorHouse™
1663 Liberty Drive
Bloomington, IN 47403 USA
www.authorhouse.co.uk
Phone: 0800.197.4150

Published by AuthorHouse   11/20/2014

ISBN: 978-1-4918-9537-5 (sc)
ISBN: 978-1-4918-9539-9 (e)

This book is dedicated to millions of factories workers who use their God-given talents and abilities to work full time and unable to lift their own families off the breadline.

CONTENTS

INTRODUCTION

This book tells a story and also serves as a guide for those who want to start or running their own business. The story is about a black guy living in Portsmouth originally from Cameroon who was student in Switzerland. It is an *inspiration moment of my life experience and the uncertainty situation I was facing in my own country in 1996 when I started my first business.*

After five years of hard work and research on Internet to build my business to earn my Financial Freedom, I felt the desire to share with you a story, 'The story of my life'.

This story comes partially from my black Africa Country, where I spent my childhood, and from the White Country where I spent most of my time studying, living and work. The language was not a barrier to my integration when I was student in Geneva where people speak French, unfortunately like many foreigners I was doing odd jobs, but this didn't stop me fighting to build my dream. By ambition, by choice or by necessity I've never asked the question. As long as human beings continue to immigrate, to move to the land of Human Being I would never ask a question.

I went to Europe through the air; my family expected a lot from me, I had to fulfill the dreams of young people of my Mother's village by building an Integrated Center of Development and Health Center. The dream was so big and I hoped that my integration would be quick and easy. Unfortunately, there are people who hate you and want you to fail. It seems that I had the winning combination of Lotto in my hand.

This is my story, this is my vision. You start your life with expectations and dreams, but as you go, life is not always as you had imagined. Life is as it is and sometime it depends on someone else. "Be yourself, Think big and Think different. Treat people with respect and dignity. Follow your dream no matter what. Make it happen, enjoy your life and live fully."

Jean T: Founder of Connecting Enterprise. Messenger of strategies. Creator of Anonymous Millionaires. Motivator of Young Entrepreneurs. People call me professor Drop Shipping

Chapter 1

THE SCANDAL OF POOR SALARY

How All this happened

In 2003 I was in London finding a new opportunity due to the advent of internet business. This was a tough moment of my life, due to the language barrier. I was a factory worker at Cooper Vision Manufacturing, a five years degree doing 48 hours per week and tow days overtime, four years later I've turndown a job of £33.000 as a consultant; the same amount of money I was earning when I was student in Switzerland in 1998-2002. Why? Because I was not there to chase a salary or any position, I wanted to be financially free. And a five years degree was not the best way for me to be financially free. So when I told friends, members of my family and some colleagues that I'm going to start a million pound Internet business plan turnover and I need 2 or 3 people to join me, people were laughing and look at me like I've lost my mind. "Hey Jean where all this money comes from, show us the money! What are you still doing in this factory if you know how to make money?"

Some of my colleagues were saying that. "This black guy has gone mad; you want to start a business when you're at the bottom ladder of this company, what a crazy black. Instead of wasting your time about starting a business, you should focus all your energy and time doing a lot of overtime. We are sure that you will stay in this company until your last day of retirement, if the company doesn't sack you before." You see they were judging me by the colour of my skin, not by the character of my contents and the know-how. So in Internet time like this, if you really know what you want to be, you will find what to do that will lead you where you want to be. Do not let yourself smothered by the ignorance of some and barren criticisms, and never let your small business make you small-minded.

Remember there are only two things that can change your life: something comes inside of you and you make it happened, or something comes out of you and you take action.

This book is the story of how I did it, of what worked well and what went wrong, my success and mistakes. The key lesson I've learnt on my journey and collectively, it is the secret formula for financial freedom in today Internet business. And this book is a crucial guide tool for anyone who wants to start a business or any business owner who wants to make it big. If you are committed to getting what you REALLY want from: your life, your business, your customers, and then you need to learn:

The Jean Secret Formula To Get Ahead: [*F^2 = (A+ V+ R) x O + (D+HW)] (F^2: Financially Free - A: Attitude - V: Vision – R: Risque - O: Opportunity - D: Dicipline - HW: HardWork). This is not a Concept and Theory, it is not a formula that will revolutionise the science, but it will help change the lives of individuals. As a consultant and someone who runs his own business, I am always focus more on Process and Practical Methodology to help our learners and entrepreneur to move directly and efficiently step by step from point A to point B to achieve a specific outcome. Because truly, one of the keys to succeed, in Internet time is *continuous learning*. In fact, it's a necessity. If you're not constantly learning, you'll simply be passed by.

People on Minimum Wage

We all have a life experience and a story that can inspire others to live a better life or run a better business. This book is some kind of answer to a system, which fails to reward effort and commitment for the millions working poor. "*Live What You Love: The 20 Golden Secrets of Business Attitudes to Succeed*" shows how you can make a difference and an income at the same time by sharing your life experience and advice with others. The book is written for everyone who has ever dreamed of living his/her life free of financial constraints, and owning his/her own business. A significant number of researches have illuminated the consequences of living on low wages. The governments only think about increasing the age of retirement, this more often than not, leave workers unable to lift their own families off the breadline and this is clearly an obscene scandal in many developed countries. Benefit cuts by government busy scything pay packet-filling tax credits while it vindictively drives down the value of wages, are an indefensible attack on the living standards of an army of factory workers and unemployed. There are many people and organisation far better qualified than politicians to ameliorate and reverse some of the most pernicious social trends in our communities that cause and perpetuate misery for too many. In other words, to believe that an army of bureaucrats can solve the problems of the under-privileged workers is to ignore the evidence of the report wrote by many organisations during the last decade. It is a cold-hearted government that gifts huge tax cuts to a wealthy so-called "Elite" then blames the unemployed for their joblessness and undermines the income of those who put in a full shift on small wages. After the slavery of black people, we have now enter the slavery of those who are victims of radical religious and slavery of employees in minimum wage who are not able to lift up their family.

I've been in the "New Deal," ten years ago a sort of bogus programme of government; which is run by Job Centre, created by some politicians who do not really care out of workers on lower incomes or unemployed. The system does not really work, except for those that have designed it to fill their pockets. In other words it works for those who are making money on the back of the government through this New Deal.

The programme is a form of punishment for the unemployed rather than a pathway to employment. This is where it is wrong, you've worked all these years yet; you get punished for being made redundant. Everybody who has been on it will testify that not just those looking for work feel let down by Job Centre, the environment is equally appalling. Whereby, users seat around doing nothing but to read newspapers that are over week-old as their source of job search, this is as demoralising and frustrating as New Deal is.

A decent day's pay for a fair day's work should be a basic entitlement to all human beings; it is a natural human desire to everybody to want to live a better life. You too will soon enter the *Club45-45-45™ or you are already in.* You will work *45* hours per week for *45* years to pay tax and bill, to receive *45* percent of what you earn now and that is not enough to live on. At the end of your working days, you will end up with nothing in your hands and die alone. Now is the time to make the biggest difference in the life of your family and yourself, no matter whether you come from homeless or disadvantaged background.

We must understand that the school only provides a "survival kit" of knowledge, a bit of everything and expert in nothing. Consider that we finished learning after school, is at best very handicapping to our life while the world continues to accelerate its course of development. Today with all the advancements in technology, knowledge, and a superior standard of living, people still live with less hope and an increased sense of deprivation in their wellbeing.

But if you look around, you see that the advent of Internet and Socials Medias is a blessing; it has reduced the whole world to a new starting point that gives everyone a new opportunity. Is it that you still waiting for the opportunities of your life? If you act today, you can claim your small piece of knowledge that could have you laughing at any money matter that you might have right now. Do not stays with what seem to be safe and let drop the opportunities, there is no longer job security anymore and you can be sack at any time. *I know a lot of people believe on security, anyway let me told you something, the only place is secure in life is prison and no one want to go there, so don't think about security, you create your security everyday by the step you take everyday.*

I found that when I was a factory worker after the death of one of our colleagues with ten years of loyal services, the company did not even mention this painful loss during the team break, even symbolically, what a shame! Most of us heard the sad new by rumours; the boss did not value him because he had no value in the market place. At the same period national TV was broadcasting the news of a missing cat that was found after ten years of disappearance. Would you like to end up like that? This is an opportunity to make the real changes in your life. Do not let someone else take your place. If it is not you who use these tools, it will be the person in front of you. This small invitation to my life story could change your career or business forever, it could change your life for better overnight and it could help you change a lot of lives too.

We have all been confronted at one time or another in our life by "fear": fear of losing a loved one, fear of losing our job, fear of embarking on a new project. But there's nothing wrong with being motivated to do something new, and it's often the kick-start that we need to get going on a new project no matter what!!

Chapter 2

MY LIFE STORY

My Childhood

Coming from the family of six girls and five boys, I grew up in a small city called Esse. It is a small town located 80 km from Yaoundé the capital of Cameroon in equatorial forest where everyone knew everyone.

My father moved to settle in this part of country in 1945 fleeing political unrest in western Cameroon. Very soon he made his name as a great photographer and gained the confidence of local authorities to produce identities photos cards for citizens. He traveled throughout the region taking pictures.

The mains activities of the population were farming: food crops and cocoa plantation. Greek companies had settled for the cocoa trade where farmers were exploited as slaves. While French companies had embarked on industrial exploitation of the forest.

The local labours were used for industrial slaughtering of trees that were soon transported to major European Countries.

No factory was created; there were no roads, no reward for the exploitation of the forest. In the eyes of the people we felt indignation and hatred. Corruption was used as a method of governing. All officials were corrupt, and it seemed normal that people resigned to complain because the complaints were put in the trash. The market was periodic and was held two times per month, during which time the farmers had to sell their products, people came from everywhere and the atmosphere was friendly, it was a moment of emotional release and joy for the oppressed and miserable peasants.

There was no electricity as in large cities, rather a generator which supplied a whole city, especially in the areas occupied by officials, French exploiting of forest and cocoa buyers. We had to walk 2 km to get drinking water from a kind of large Water Wells Constructed by French expatriates. It was a hassled to get water because there was a huge crowd between 5am to 7am and 4pm to 6pm; everyone wants to be served in first place. This engendered fights, because by the time the water dried up.

Being Catholic Christians as was my dad, we had to travel every Sunday 4km on foot to get to the church built outside the city. Each of my brothers and sisters received 25 or 30 cents from our dad, which allowed us to purchase sugar cane, lollipops or fritter. These 25 or 30 cents were so inspiring that we forget we had 4km of walking to do on a sweltering heat or light rain.

We lived there when I was very young. I was raised and educated like many in modern society to believe that life is about the improvement of mankind for the on-going advancement of our planet. My father used to say: "Jean go to school, study hard, get good degree and you will find a high-pay job with great benefits". I do remember when our house burned into ashes and we lost everything, and it was not until later in life that I discover how tough we had to deal with life.

The purpose of this golden book is not to convince you to start an online business or some kind of business. I don't judge, but I'm just asking the questions, is up to you to make a judgement and that is your entirely decision. Having been researching on Internet for many years when I was a factory worker and built **connecting-enterprise.co.uk** that was started by me as an anonymous entrepreneur and joined by a team member of the same vision, this book is an *inspiration programme of my life experience*, and has nothing to do with university course or college course. I'm not some professors or consultants who've never risked a penny of their own money, the information contained here are things that happened to me and everything I talk about in this book to do we've already tested in many businesses. I am an entrepreneur who's here to help to avoid the common traps that I've fallen into. Moreover, to sensitise you on the prevalence of scammers that are out there and give you the true information instead of relying on rumours. If you are currently unhappy with the amount of your revenue, that is time to act.

This book is my effort to pull back the curtains of my business and invite you in, whenever you will decide to quit the *Club45-45-45, where you work 45 hours per week for 45 years as slave for money to pay tax and bills, to receive 45% of what you earn now, which is not enough to sustain your living standard, then to be in financial slavery for your personal debts.*

Remember if you are between twenty five and thirty years old you only have 21,000 days left to live. Now take a pencil eraser, look your payslip and your age; ask yourself how long it would take you to save £200,000 would the bank agree to pay you 15% interest on your saving of £415 a month? It is about 40 years and you have to pay £20,000 in tax if they pay you the principal. And £20,000 paid over 40 years is a little over £100,000 in income.

The Story behind my Financial Freedom

My dad was a photographer, farmer and trader; he was known by his nickname *Daniel the Millionaire*. And yet, when I was fifteen years old I saw our house burned into the ashes due to a faulty generator that my Dad was using in his photo studio. That day we lost everything, I say we have lost all our wealth; going from the higher middle class family to the corridors of poverty and that was very hard to live with even for a fifteen year-old, as I was then. My Dad was very troubled by this incident as he was the sole breadwinner, not to mention the accumulation of bills that were awaiting him. *I remember my dad sitting on the floor counting every coin and telling me about his tax, bill and debt worries. He used to send me to the door to tell the tax collector he was not in.*

My Mum had health problems and could not care for us and was sent back to her biological parent's where there was no healthcare. My siblings and I experienced the frustrations of having to cook and to do everything by ourselves, people around us were compassionate hypocrisy and they were so happy of our miserable new situation.

Following the difficulties that our family was enduring, my little brother Ambrose and I took the responsibility of contributing for the entire life of family. I had to combine my studies with domestic work and Ambrose decided to drop out of school and became a hunter, laying traps in the bush, so that we can have something to eat at home. Unlike Ambrose and I who decided to stay in our family house, our elder siblings went to live with uncles or aunts. Despite the fact that I was fifteen at the time, this tragedy allowed me to understand that we live in a world of hypocrisy where true friends are rare. As sad as this experience was though, it was a pivotal moment in my life.

Since that event I started thinking differently, I was born again; I know what means not being able to provide something to your love ones. From that day, I realised that people around me had not changed because of our circumstances. The sun was still shining, the neighbours still continue to take care of their daily routine, and the earth continues to revolve around the sun. It was my personal circumstance and environment that had changed. Just because of the house of my family had burned; this did not mean that the world had fallen apart. Life was still going on, and even in a better way for others. Eventually I found myself living in a poor condition. One day, I was sitting on a wooden bench at the middle of the sweaty air and nervous, outside, the ground was heavy and the sky had shade and texture of soggy porridge. As I stood there thinking about what to do, it hit me that my father was not wrong, he had worked so hard for what he had achieved, my mum was sent back to his village where there was no hospital, I felt robbed and cheated by life. It was not just the house that burned, but the whole family was in danger of burning too.

I was on the verge of breaking down. I had sworn to never be short of money in my entire life, I set up my goal to be financially free.

In fact I always asked this question to people: do you live fully or do you survive? Are you living where you want to live and at the standard of living you want to live at? This is time to change your life and I will show you how. In this light, I shall be focusing on what I think was important for me, changing people lives with my life story. But when I wake up each morning I had no idea how to bring my dream into a reality.

I knew there was a lot of work to do, in order to get myself ready. I also asked myself, who would want to listen even in my community? Who will listen to an unknown Black African man an immigrant for that matter? Who was not brought up in the UK's cultural system and yet, he talk about life inspiration? Who would listen even I knew how to inspire others, train, motivate and transform people's life or how to get my message out there? Well, I must be a crazy black man. I just wanted to share with people what I knew about life experience, but I was limited by the perception that people might have on me as a black person and also on the fact that, some might judge me by the colour of my skin rather than the content of my message. I remember vividly what my Dad used to tell me, "Jean everything you told me is not written in books". And yet my father did not know that he had just inspired me to write what I knew in books. Really, my father did not want me to contradict him, due to African culture which postulates that; we must respect our parents regardless of the circumstances because they know best. He did not want to lose his parental authority in front of a child, even if what I was saying was true.

Today it would be a bit exaggerated to suggest that I started connecting-enterprise.co.uk or create-to-succeed.co.uk to solve the problems of society; but it would be true to say that I started it because I wanted to solve a "problem inside Cameroonian's community, living in Portsmouth in England. The problem of being constantly in front of people that were having significant language barriers in terms of basic communication and integration as well as those who wanted to start their business. That is where my motivation started, I knew that in any community there are people with *The Know-How*, but they need a little help. I am not a writer. Perhaps I cannot write my story skilfully, but I am writing with complete truthfulness as my foundation.

Back in March of 2005 I had decided I wanted to create a Mastermind Group, I had founded Portsmouth Cameroonian Association and African Cultural Organisation for Integration, with the aim of motivating people how to turn their idea into fruition, how to get out of state benefit and how to create their own financial freedom. I learned to talk to people of many nationalities coming from a disadvantaged or homeless background who like me, were searching for a better life. Every week I was in the street distributing a leaflet and flyers to people to join me to form a group. Even at my workplace I was handing out leaflets to my colleagues detailing how to start a social enterprise as an entrepreneur, but no one was really interested. My message and leaflets were falling on "deaf ears and blind eyes". My logic did not fit their logic; the problem was that my logic was the logic of the 1% of smart people who talk about ideas, but not for average people who talk about event, those who were looking for job and promotion, or dumb people who talk about other people.

Later in the month I attended a seminar in Brighton with the focus on creating of community groups and how to raise fund. Fresh from that seminar, I started writing projects to present to the different funding organisations. As a result, I met dozens of investors and successful entrepreneurs in seminar unfortunately many lenders turned me down citing lack of referral.

In 2007 I started doing my own research in the Internet. Fortunately I came across a mentor, someone who was passionate about life inspiration. His speech was recorded on online video, and if I had not really discovered this, I would never have been able to bring this project to fruition; it would have died in my dreams.

I know what I'm saying might sound stupid, but the guy was speaking the language that I seemed to understand, his name is *Christian Godefroy*. Christian was helping people with what he knows about life experience and I wanted to follow in his footsteps but from my own life experiences. The day I received his video training programme, called *"Simple ways to succeed on the Internet"*. I listened to the programme over and over from when I was going to bed or when I was waking up in the morning. The concepts in the programme were stunning for a man like me to hear, it was clearly a reminder of what I have to do in my life, control my destiny, make a new decision, let my vision guide me, live fully with passion and make it happen. I can say without any hesitation that his online video training programmes added something new in my life.

Another one was *Brendon Burchard*, his speech was upload on online video, a free training called "*The Million Dollars Business Plan*," In the months that followed, I bought the entire Brendon Burchard books, *The Millionaire Messenger*, *The Charge* etc, knowing that I could not afford to attend his seminars in United State of America. I listened to his audio; video and read his book and started practicing myself. I also read the books written by Robert T. Kiyosaki: *Rich Dad Poor Dad—Cash flow Quadrant—Increase Your Financial IQ*. I listened video and audio sent to me by Christian Godefroy direct marketing expert. I put in the practice what they were saying to do even I have never met some of these experts, they are mentors for me, I learn from them and I still learning. I trained myself in the areas of entrepreneurship, personal development and financial education. I also plane to read new practical books every week.

My live as an employee

During my short lifetime as a factory worker with minimum wage, I was working 12 hours a day, 7am to 7pm, four days per week, plus one or two days overtime in a Contact Lens Company. My day starts with a loud sound of an alarm clock at 5:30 am to wake me up. I have to travel 20 miles 6 days/week to my workplace at Hamble in the city of Southampton in England.

I still remember sitting in my cold tiny room at Portsmouth in 2007, asking myself:

Hey Jean what do you want to be? What are you doing in this cold place without any heater in the room?

My first answer was:

- I want to inspire other people and be financially free *smart.*

The second answer was:

- I do not want an alarm clock, which is ringing at 5:30 am to wake me up or work 70 hours a week.
- The last one was: guy Live What You Love and make it happen.

As an employee, whatever I was saying: "I see with my mind what other people might miss with their eyes" people around me; friends or relatives were laughing, some of my colleagues were laughing at me, saying: hey guy what are you still doing here at the bottom ladder of the company if you really have this vision? Rather than wasting your time thinking about creating your business, why not apply for a position to be AB2 or XY4? We are sure you will still be here for thirty years-time working at the bottom ladder of this company. The more they were said it the more I became motivated. In other words, their negative comments were like an engine in my powerful computer '*My Brain*'. I started planning to write my golden Book "*Live 'What You Love: The 20 Golden Secrets Formula of Business Attitudes to Succeed*" in order to inspire other people, who think like me, when I was managing my online business, without quitting my factory day job.

Around this time 5 years ago (2010) I started to experiment with online marketing in the hopes to bring in a supplemental income to help buy a new land, the university fees for my wife and her living expenditures. I was already working full time and over time making money to live, but the reason why I wanted to make *more* was because I was going to be *broke* with the fee of my wife's university and other miscellaneous in Switzerland. I did not want to get a part time job at another company to pay for her studies, it would have made me pay more tax on my income, and get a pittance at the end.

So, when I started, I was waking up at 5:30 am, going to my regular job, coming home at 7:30pm and then I would work on my online business from 09:00pm to 01:00am. Then wake up at 5:30 am for work again the next day.

I was busting my ass everyday trying to get this online thing to work and I was working two jobs, my regular job plus my online business. I was doing everything myself, from the design, to the marketing, to the copywriting and videos coupled with the fact that I did not know how, I would train myself through hours of Google researches with lot of frustration when things were going wrong. My wife Debora Helene was studying pharmacy in Switzerland; she was not there, even when my wife was there during school holidays, herself looked no better. Her outstandingly pretty face was ravaged by too much stress of her own coursework, too much worry and by too many disturbed nights caused by a baby who only seemed sleep when she was holding him. No one was there to partner with me or to show me what to do. Fortunately Internet was there with lots of forum where I could ask people who share the same vision for help, it took me many years, but it was worth it and this is the result.

You see if I've learned one thing over the years, it's that all achievers have one thing in common. We can feel isolate and alone. Most of the people around us in our daily lives, whether it's at work, or friends and family, don't share our burning desire to succeed. If you're trying to start or grow a business, that goes double. I know that because I was like you seven years ago. Most of the people around me thought I was mad and some did not hesitate to share their criticism. I had never felt so abandoned and so lost in all my life. In fact I know I never would have made it if I hadn't had a group of like-minded people that could lean on for advice and encouragement.

In today's Internet Time and Social Media, it is not so much what you know anymore that counts, because often what you know is old. It is how fast you can learn a new skill that is priceless. Things are constantly changing in our world today and working hard for money is and old formula born in the day of industrial time. Opportunities are shifting and methods that worked in the past simply do not work anymore. *Nowadays it's impossible for any single person to keep up with them.* The most successful changes I've made in my business were as a resulted of things shared by member of my mastermind group, and there really isn't a better way to grow and learn because you're effectively learning from other people's experiences, mistakes and success.

So while I watch many people trying to achieve success on their own, the rich know how to get richer and those on the outside get left out, and you know that, that's a truth as old as life itself, the insiders win every time.

For many years I was unhappy, sometimes downright miserable, about my work I was in the wrong place. I felt underutilised and I knew I was underpaid. And interestingly, this happened both while I was working for Cooper Vision England and while I was selling Mary Kay product and Shoes during my four days off. Then one day something changed, it was my *mindset*. I was pitching my products to a potential client when I realised that the people in the room were much more interested in what I knew than what I was selling. It was at that point that, I realised that I should stop selling stuff and start selling what I know.

In my work place, some of our colleagues were crying, in their eyes I saw the distress and the light that fills the place. It looks like they were born to suffer; it seems that happiness was prohibited. Are we doomed to search our entire lives without finding anything?

You too will soon enter the ***Club45-45-45***™. You will work 45 hours per week for 45 years to receive 45% of what you earn now and that is not enough to live with. At the end of your working days, you will be alone with nothing in your hands. Is it that you still waiting for the opportunities of your life? Breaks the rules, decides your future, choose how, when to work and especially how much to earn?

How by playing the lottery? You will need a lot of luck, around one in thirteen millions! By playing in casino and bet? You'll make others people more rich. How by investing in the stock market? This is not the right moment! By creating your own business? Although you'll need a great investment, if not you will need to find a Sugar dad or a Sugar mum!

Indeed I offer you something simple, efficient and effective the Drop shipping and fulfilment by Amazon, the best way to win and get out of anonymity and become your own boss, no longer angry with a manager who dictates what you do even when you're right. Take advantage of the advent of Internet to make money and a lot of money. Do not live the dreams of others, do not depend on agenda of someone else, but decided to realise yours, for you and for all those who are important to you in life.

Do not lose more time, you're at the right place to get out of *Club45-45-45* and avoid what is said in investors meeting: "*what can we do to motivate our workers to work harder and be more loyal without paying them more*". Decide when to attend a new-training seminar to learn how to earn money with Online Business and quit the conventional rat race of life or the Club45-45-45.

I continued to work hard for my Business, even after making 05 times my salary in 01 month I didn't quit my job. I had planned to leave the Club45-45-45 in the month that my lovely wife Debora will graduate in pharmacy; so we can celebrate together our success. To my friends and colleagues it was a joke, for them I had no alternative, except to stay my whole life at the bottom level of the company. It was petty but it was making me smile more than anything because that had shown how much what these people thought of me.

I can't believe it's been that long, seven years. It seems like only seven days I was putting up blogs, building back links, creating products and doing everything myself, I was dedicated, I was motivated and I was driven. Seven years later all I can say is that I'm so incredibly grateful for everything that my online business has done for my family's lives and me. There is no way I could have made it through all the mistakes I went, if I did not have my support group there to remind me of my dream and keep the fire burning. And even though I've gone onto create L.W.Y.L and enjoy massive success, I still count my Mastermind group as one of my biggest assets. Nowadays, I no longer have to wake up at 5:30 am and this was one of the first things to do when I left from the conventional rat race of life.

Now, I know something about: there's something that you know too, or are interested in researching and reporting on, that other people are willing to pay money to know. It may be something about how to be a better parent, how to have a successful marriage even though you're a child of divorce family, or how to deal with the loss of a loved one. It could be something about business—How to be a better marketer, leader or how to write a story. It could be something about health and wellness—How to lose weight, how to beat depression, or how to control diabetes. It could be a tough experience that you've had somewhere in your life that you learned how to overcome. There's something that people ask you about all the time, or that you find yourself advising other people about constantly. That's a huge opportunity for you! Your life's story, your professional experience and unique message to the world are valuable beyond your imagination.

Businesses, governments, politicians and all leaders use storytelling. You can make an extraordinary difference and a fortune sharing your advice with the world. Who you are and what you know can be leveraged, packaged and monetized through books, speeches, seminars, or online marketing.

As an entrepreneur, my duty is *to inspire, train, motivate and transform* those who want to succeed and grow their business. If I managed to do it, you can make it too, even better than me. If you read the biography of rich or wealthy people around the world, you will find that 98% of them were average and ordinary people like you, some on minimum wage, they did not start rich. But like anything else, there is some training in order to avoid problems. There is no shortcut for success and this golden book has nothing to do with getting rich quick. It is the Bible of Internet Drop-shipping Business and Fulfilment By Amazon, to show you how to fish in the simple professional way with all the tools. You need to add only 15% of your own energy and sacrifice 5% of your time; those are just the 20% who provide 80% of all the success you need to be financially free.

I think today, the opportunities for huge success have never been bigger. In every single field there are revolutionary breakthroughs almost every single day. The number of new millionaires created in the next few years will be unprecedented in the history of the world. But we all know, and to some degree, we have all felt the effects of the economic crisis across the world in the last few years. Some people have been hit so hard that they've lost the desire to dream, hoping instead just to survive. To those we must bring even more hope and encouragement, along with a fresh set of ideas that will fire their dreams again.

This Step-by-Step-Workbook offers you an opportunity to make a real change in your life, whether you are a new into the business-world or have been in it for a while. Do not let someone else take your place. If it is not you who is using those tools, its will be the person in front of you. This book provides you with everything you need to know, a step-by-step guide in starting online business. The course is structured in a logical way; anybody can do this, just follow the step-by-step process and procedure written in this book. I have used *The 20 Golden Secrets of Business attitude to Succeed* and it has enabled me to be where I am today. Use your spare time and vacation to copy me and do your homework, think big, think different, set your goal no matter what people say and make it happen.

As I stated previously there is no shortcut to success, "failing to prepare is preparing to fail". Quick resolution does not work for your smoking problems at hospital, it does not work for your career promotion, it does not work for your particular weight loss and it probably will not work for your business. If you really want to make money on the Internet, you have to put down the *reality TV show, stop procrastinate and pack away every distractions.* You must leave your «self-sabotage behaviours» and enter the real business world. The truth is not always pretty, but it needs to be known. There are two business worlds out there: The dreamer's business world and the real business world.

We know that it never an easy task to create or start any business. The information in this book is not for those who are expecting a shortcut solution to succeed. Many want-to-be entrepreneurs are looking for something so easy, without any effort, little investment and little time. They will find their own money-tree-machine or start a reality TV show. If you are interested about starting a business, but need a little help to break the glace, you will be delighted with this easy training programme that is not only cheap but tailor-made for you and will enable you to start online business, add video or audio in your website, without any knowledge on web design. It's like planting a tree; you water it for years and then one day it doesn't need you anymore. Its roots are deeply driven into the ground, and the tree provides shade for your happiness.

The information contained here are the result of years of hard work, Internet researches, marketing, and experience of running my own enterprise. These are intended to help you to avoid the mistakes I made in the past before finding the right people. I just do not want you to believe in what I am saying, but I want you to practice it yourself, you can do it! This small invitation to www.create-to-succeed.co.uk could change your career or business forever, and it could change your life for better overnight.

Chapter 3

FINANCIAL VISIONS

The illusion of being rich

Most people think that working hard for money and then going out to buy things that make them look wealthy will miraculously make them rich, but in most cases it does not. It only makes them more tired, they call it "keeping up with the joneses" and if you notice, the joneses are exhausted. Most of this happened in some communities where some people want to be what they are not. Instead of working hard to pay tax and bills, it is better to work hard to acquire assets. As reminder to you, I started with little money and that several banks turned me down. Web designers were charging me a lot at that time, the training programmes were so long and complicated to understand. I eventually got in contact with some physically and started my Drop Shipping Internet home base business. I have never been addicted to the idea of a high-paying job. I have work in factory for twelve hours shift every day and having to stand up for at least ten hours. But I choose to do it in order to enhance my vision of financial freedom. I have always wanted to develop a pattern of thinking that focuses only in assets and income from business and royalties. In the Internet time, people who still choose to do physically and demanding work will always have less pay and this has been the case throughout history and it still the case today.

Today when I meet people who are worried about paying their bills, some get frustrated with me because they ask me to tell them the magic formula how they can make money; they do not like the idea of following *The 20 Golden Secrets of Business Attitudes to Succeed*. They do not like the idea of learning a new skill or thinking long-term. Many are desperately seeking a shortcut solution because they have money problems that needs be solved right now. They have the idea of owning a big house, holidays, big cars, eating out in nice restaurants, going to fancy nightclubs and getting married when they are still young. Many are fixated upon the shortcut to getting rich quick. In other words, they want quick answers on what *to do* instead of hearing what needs to *be* done in order to acquire their financial freedom. To these people, I wish them luck to build their own money-tree-machine, for their financial freedom.

You should know that I saw all our belongings burn after the fire at our house. The only property that remained to us was a house in the capital and a cocoa plantation; later on it was recovered by the autochthones following a serial of corruption. In my country of origin called Cameroon, corruption had reached an unbearable level. The government and public service are full of mediocre intellectuals, those who are there to kill the country. Head of State, Ministers, army officers, directors of companies and the rich sent their children to study in Europe or in America. Those who could not study there will spend their holidays over there. While the local media broadcast to poor parents the advantages of sending their children to spend holidays in the countryside or villages. These false and contradictory speeches of our leaders have made me become aware. This is how I decided to pursue my studies in Europe, and particularly in Switzerland in order not to find myself in a system where corruption is a model for those who run the country. No progress would have been possible for people like me if I were still in Cameroon.

Late in 2009, I came across a friend of mine who is a Swiss citizen of Africa origin. It was 2: 00am in a summer month during the Geneva festivities. Mario was sitting on a bench in the public park called 'Les Promenades Anglaises', a very nice place with a big clock on the floor, head bowed, while slowly twirling his car key in his hand and wearing a tired and dejected expression. Mario had never been particularly an emotional person, but at this moment he did not know what to feel. He was too numb to be angry, the silence and emptiness in the dark park mirrored his heart at that moment. Until now life, had been very well, he had a good job, a fairly nice house and the kids had not brought the police or a yob knocking on his door. Suddenly, the loss of concentration, the keys slipped from his hands and fell on the ground with a clank. He didn't make a move quickly to pick them up; instead he lifted his head and stared at the blue navy Lamborghini that was parked in the side road. What was the use of having an expensive flash car like that now? A sudden feeling of deep coldness came over him, causing a shiver to cut right through. Mario bowed his head again, and cupped his hands in a prayer manner.

But nothing like this had ever happened to him before, I saw a wave emotion came over him and the tears streamed down his face. Mario did not notice the figure of my shadow walking towards him. I stood quietly for a minute, wondering whether to talk to him or walk away.

Finally I broke the silence. Hi Mario! How are you here so late? My voice caught him completely off guard, causing him to jump slightly as he turned towards me with a startled expression on his face. Mario instantly recognised me, but he did not want to respond and kept in his original position. I did not have to be an angel to recognise that here was a man in desperate time, so by the lack of response, I gently put my hand on Mario's shoulder and said "You look as you've lost your mother or thing fall a part, is everything all right"? Again Mario held his silence, although he had known me for many years when we were student, we also worked together in a restaurant before he got a high-pay job. He always asked me what I was doing in the factory instead of looking for a high-pay job; but he just wanted to be left a lone. I did not take the hint; I choose to sit down beside him. "Is there anything I can do to help"? My friend was screaming his head, "Hey! Go away and leave me alone. Can't you mind your own business and let me have my breakdown in peace? I will be fine, thank you." I slowly stood and replied with care, I will give you some room, I am sorry to have disturbed you. I started to walk across 'Les Promenades Anglaises' in the dark empty park. Mario followed me, "I'm sorry I did not want to be so rude. In my mind I wanted to be a lone, in my heart I knew, I need to speak to someone like you". I returned where we were, but remained standing, I do understand what you're enduring, and I have been there myself. But let's go somewhere, there is a nice restaurant just around the corner, and I think we would be better there. We walked out of the public park after a few minute we entered the restaurant. On arrival at front door Mario, who was still completely absorbed could not notice the name on the doorplate 'Mind Your Spending Habits', strange name for a restaurant Mario remarked.

Once inside I ordered two cups of coffee, Mario asked me if I am still working in the factory. I had told him, it is my road for the financial freedom, I need more time for my family and for myself. My wife was a student in pharmacy at university of Geneva. This architect makes more than £55,000 a year with big home and a holiday house in Barbados, three cars a Lamborghini, a Jaguar and a family car with a beautiful family of four children. He told me that, he is always in some sort of financial trouble. He pulled out a piece of paper from his pocket opened it and gave it to me to read, it was his wife letter and it reads:

Dear sweetheart,

I don't know how to start, where to start and what to say. But I know we've been together for 13 years and our life have not been so bad. For a long time I'm not longer motivated emotionally and intellectually by our lifestyle even our relationship. We have worked so hard for what we have achieved.

Life in the early days wasn't easy for us. We had little money, two children, I have to do extra cleaning jobs and you had to study long hours to get where you are today. For a while now, there has been a lack of intimacy and trust between us, due to your commitments you seem incapable of seeing this and we've grown apart, our four children are growing up.

I don't completely blame you for this situation, but I need more, open your eyes, if we carry on our lifestyle like this we would end up empty handed at the end of our working day.

That's why I've decided to stay away from home a while on my own, to try and put things in order. I don't know how long for, take care of our children, but I will contact you.

I am so sorry

Your lover Angelina"

Having read this letter, I asked my friend if I could have a look at his bank statement and I found that, he had a financial sickness and that would be terminal if he lost his job or if he did not change his spending habits. May be not, I am not sure that Angelina has left you because she does not love you, but because she thinks you won't understand and you would try to persuade her to continue as you live. She ends up feeling she has nothing of real value or worth to pass on to her children and their children. Mario fails to realise that it is not how much money he makes that was important, but how much he could save and how many generation he could keep it for. It just goes to show how important financial planning is and that you shouldn't leave inheritance issues until later life—nobody expects to die young but it happens.

It always amazes me that they don't give more time to this stuff in schools. Because it's not in the government's interest to educate people on how to plan finances sensibly and avoid these sorts of disasters. If they did, the government would get a lot less money.

My advice to him was simple: "guy you need to sit down and map out a plan to get control of your spending habits" echoing the message his wife was sending to him. If you need help, ask for an assistance of some financial adviser. They can help you to layout a plan where you can improve your personal expenses.

4

My Sad Experience

Indeed, if you have never heard of me, I am like many anonymous entrepreneurs, I wrote a lot of projects, I have even met a housemate a Netherlander, an employee working with the navy as welder originally from Ghana and a mechanic by trade. I spoke to him on several occasions about starting a business together. I asked him to list the materials we need to start a *"workshop of car repaired for exportation to Africa, specialised on changing the steering wheel from the right to the left"*. There was a huge market for this project, but the guy dropped my proposal and three months later he started his own car-repaired garage, the same thing I told him. Nineteen months afterward, he abandoned his business, he could not serve customers alone and he could not deliver on time. The reality is that, he was not prepared to start this business. He just copied my project and tried to implement it because he was a mechanic. In doing so, he was violating the natural laws of the universe, he wanted to get rich quick and alone. He did not want a partner, share his knowledge or train other.

As Dee Lee pointed out that, "Our selfishness does not allow us to work together on projects to achieve common outcomes, because when we are together, our ego dominates our common goals, and all our organisations just seem to promote our names, without making real change in our lives".

Here is another disappointment. Having found that people were more interested in what I was saying, than what I was selling to them, I took the initiative to delegate the sale of my goods to my little brother Michel in Cameroon, who kept asking me that he was ready to engage in a business with me. At the same time my niece Solange living in Dijon, France offered me the same proposal, she wanted to sell Mary Kay products.

Following the interest that these two people had expressed, I did not hesitate a moment to engage with them in this business so that I can concentrate on create-to-succeed. co.uk my training website on Drop Shipping Business and Fulfilment By Amazon. During that time, my brother had promised to find offices to expand the business. But this relationship has turned into a nightmare for my business, despite all the expenses I incurred to ship the goods to my brother in Cameroon and my niece in Dijon, this without mentioning the training that I paid to help them develop in sales and online marketing. I've never had any news for them, but I was surprised to hear that Michel moved to Nigeria with all the money, and my niece has never responded to my phone call. No news of them, no contact during two years. And yet I continue to believe that they will come with some good news. However, I had just being abused and swindled by members of my family, the same thing I was facing in the pass by another nephew Ndoumou Richards. Until today they have never bother or say something or to get in touch with me.

Life in the early days wasn't easy, we had a little money and my wife had to study long hours to finish her last year to get where she is today. The little money I had was evaporated in the project with my financial predators. Sadly this come when we just have a new baby, I became very depressed, believing that I had let my wife down. My vision for the future to build a secure family became just a shattered dream. In the end, the stress and the disappointment were too much for me. Yes it was very painful for me, but especially for my wife who had never really wanted me to engage in any business with my family member, knowing the problem that I had with my first business The Computer & Technical Education Centre where I had been abused ten years ago.

As sad as this experience was though it was another blow in my life. I don't believe that I was wrong in trying to pass on a lasting legacy to my family by creating a business and quit the Club45-45-45. But this led me to ask the question, "What if the basis of my life vision was incorrect"? I began to wonder what the real meaning and importance of my life was, and what I wanted to leave my family with. When I lost my business and my money in such circumstances, for a while I was angry and bitter. I had worked so hard for what I wanted to achieve. I felt robbed and cheated by my relative once again. A lot of that periode was quite hazy for my wife and I. It was, I think at that time that I started a journey of rebuilding my life on something different. Over the coming months I began to concentrate more on my internet business to build on solid ground not on ground that is full of flaws and bad roots.

Another case; a friend of mine has set up a fish-farming project for an amount of £15,000 initially. Residing in

Australia, he approached his old friends and the best in the domain in his country of origin, Cameroon. Some of them have responded to him by saying that, "You want to get rich on our backs". The human being is unpredictable, he even offered them to take shares in his business, but was told, "Come and do it yourself".

This is to highlight how jealous people are when it comes to making a difference. People also hate their friends, cousins even their own brother just because they see that they will succeed in what they are doing. As a newbie entrepreneur a few years ago, I was in the same situation looking for a simple way to get my business off, following the failure of the first company.

In fact in my new project, my first website had never been released to the public before disappearing. There is nothing more frustrating to see your project failed before it gets started. After several months creating a complicated website, unable to handle it, I was the only one to visit it; I dropped down the whole computing with frustrations. Why? Because I did not have a strategy to my new business: all the skill, the team in other word the mechanism that makes a business to run.

While my entourage who already complains of time I spend on the project, does not necessarily see the results or not knowing that my own brother, nephew and niece have abused me and let me without any capital. In addition to a business that does not sell is like a "Sword of Damocles hanging over your head." This is why I decided never to fall into that trap since the failure of this business. I focused on the writing of this book and the strategy of the new project.

Few months later I had a manuscript as well as my strategy but all of this was in disorder in my laptop, iMac and USB key. I had problems to fix the content properly in order; I was not a writer until I find a minded people. In this book, I have shared with you an experience that allowed me to get where I am today. My story is not unique, may be you have one that you can share with the world. Anyway: there are thousands of people earning real money from doing drop shipping, eBay auction or selling items on Amazon. Some people just want to own their own business, myself included. I want a complete change for financial freedom.

With a well thought out survey, you can kill two birds with one stone. On one side, you have a market survey to find out what inexpensive product to sell and how to sell your product. Distribute this survey to good and reliable contacts. What concrete action plan can you follow to finally take off your activity? This is why I decided to implement the training site: www.create-to-succeed.co.uk.

If today you have moved in all directions and you feel lost, it is because you have been putting hands into all kinds of tools that have nothing to do with your first goals. If you really want to start your project, then I am asking you to bring a shovel along with me to learn how to dig towards financial freedom. In other words, I propose a simple method by going straight to the point, to reach your goal. Be careful! It is necessary to deprive yourself for a while and put aside all the other tools that prevent you from moving forward. When someone starts new business, it is normal to make mistakes and if you learn some thing new, you are then required to make mistakes in order to fully understand what you have learned. But the problem is that when people start a new business, they want to have 101 customers even though they do not know how to get one. When you have the first customer you will find that the second one is more comfortable, there is no magic formula to using drop-shipping method that I have proposed in order to start your online business or test your ability.

5

When Things go Wrong, Who do You Become?

I remember when I use to work in a factory, one of my colleagues, a woman from Scotland; she was complaining every day, when she was lame she loved to blame me, I was the problem. This meant that her emotional pain from her lower wage disappointment, or her loneliness was so strong that she wanted to push the pain onto someone else via blame. I had been chosen to be blame, but no matter what she was saying it was as if "the dog is barking the caravan goes". Whenever I meet people who are afraid to try something new, in most cases the reason lie in their fear of being disappointed, get reject by their friends, family or colleague. If you are ready to stop working all your life as a slave for money and be in financial slavery to your personal debt, I would like to give you the same words of lesson I learned from one of my mentors Robert T. Kiyosaki who said that, when you are new in business: "be prepared to be disappointed".

Instead of avoiding disappointment, be prepared for it. The disappointment, is an important part of learning process just as we learn from our mistakes, we gain character from it. Only fools expect everything to go the way they want.

They want to violate the natural laws of the universe; they are looking for a shortcut solution to financial freedom. We have seen people out there with great new business ideas. Six months later their excitement is diminished and all you hear from them is: "This idea was not good enough, I am sorry I could not carry on".

It is not that the idea did not work. It was the disappointment of being impatient. They allowed their impatience to turn into disappointment and to defeat them. Some times, this impatience is the result of them not receiving in their bank account the money they were expecting. Many people never start projects because they are waiting the answer to come from someone, they do not have themselves the answer. You will never have all the answers, no one can promise you the answer, just start no matter what. In short, we all make mistakes, we all feel upset and disappointed when things do not go our way. Yet the reason is everything is not under our control, can you stop your company from closing down, or do you have the power to stop economic crisis? Let do what you can do. In the other side, business owners or investors may wait for years to see any Cash Flow from their business or investment; they go into business with the knowledge that success may take time. They also know that good results come in slowly, and when success is achieved the reward of financial freedom will be well worth.

6

The Game has Change

Globalisation has come. You shall no longer be competing solely with the classmate you see around you. You have competitors in Cape Town, Dubai, Yokoyama, Sao Paolo, Los Angeles, Auckland, Cambridge, and Hong Kong. You will be competing with them for education, scholarships, jobs, business and even info. TV, mobile phones, newspapers, magazines and Internet have exploded in the world. But the point is you have been left out, do you remember when you last read a newspaper? The last time you opened a book was it in school? Do not lag behind for too long. You are competing with seven (7) billion souls. Despite the Orientation Law of Education, many people leave school without any qualification, a situation that creates unemployment and financial difficulties, these remains a stumbling block too many and government no longer have powers to protect and favour, only the strong shall survive. And bear in mind that, your competitors are heavily armed. In Britain 3 out of 4 persons own a Mobile phone. Internet access is easy and common as rice and stew at Christmas. 80% of the population read a weekly magazine, 30% read daily newspaper and student/youth newspapers flourish like flowers. In that country, the reading density is high. Student read up to a dozen of non-schoolbooks per year!

Information has monetary value. So what do you rely on for vibes? Rumours, be aware! The rumour is a trademark. When it passes from one person to another, each adds its own to the point where in the long run, it is not the same as its starting point. In an age like this one, information cannot be borrowed. Borrowing is like the Prime Minister leaking out a secret to a terrorist. As Shakespeare once said, "the world is a theatre, be the actor of your life!"

Employed as Production Operator in a manufacturing company, I was in a multicultural environment, I had

English, Polish, African, Caribbean and Asians, working together and it was really the globalization of work. In my team I was the only black and I was subject to a silent discrimination. Although our team leader has developed a work programme, some colleagues reserved for me the tasks they did not want to do. At first I thought of teamwork where we had to work hand in hand, but I quickly became disillusioned. I should have complained, but what would have served my complaint? I realised that my colleagues judge me by the colour of my skin and not by the content of my character. One day during a conversation some Polish girl were complaining why they did not have a permanent job? While a black man had a permanent job! At the mean time British people were not happy of loosing their job in favour of migrants. This would have led me to complain, but it had no effect on me, having worked during my studies in Geneva in a multicultural environment like this, it made me stronger to accomplish the creation of my business.

In another way, some of my colleagues were trying to show me, how they were growing in the company, they have promotion, going from production operator to technical operator or to team leader. I was not interested by their promotion; I did not need any promotion or responsibility. They were judging my background, not my ability of transforming their way of thinking. At the end I notice that they were born to be employee and nothing was wrong from them to think so. But they were missing with their eyes what I was seeing with my mind: a lot of opportunities. Simply ask yourself how many years it would take you to save £200,000 would the bank agree to pay you 20% interest on your saving? Work is like the prayer of the slave, the harder you work the more you pay taxes to the government. Many workers will have noting at the end of their working days.

Whenever I was telling people I've abandoned a proposal as a consultant, in a consulting business to work Monday to Saturday with a salary of £ 33,000 per year to the benefit of working in the factory, which allowed me to have four days off per week and devote myself to the realisation of my dream: that of being financially free. They often had to look at me like I have lost my mind. Many looked at me and said, man you will suffer here and die poor because you have committed the great stupidity of your life, £33,000 a year? You are a sick man! Something I had never said to my wife fearing that she might react negatively in line with many blockers of dreams and 90% of the population that have been trained at school and continues to be train to join the *Club45-45-45* or seek employment. Those, who will work all their life as slave for money, to be in financial slavery for personal debts and would end up, empty handed at the end of their working days in the lonely home with less than £150 per week.

I was just following the thought of James Grover Thurber "Do not look back in anger, or ahead with fear, but around you with consciousness". They often say what makes you think you can do it? Or if your idea it is so good, how comes someone else has not done it? I always reply that, because I am not someone else. Or that will never work; you do not know what you are doing. Eleanor Roosevelt said it is best to "Do what you feel in your heart to be right for, you will be criticised anyway, you will be damned if you do, and damned if you do not".

Chapter 4

GIVING BACK TO THE COMMUNITY

Looking for Opportunity

How can I show you how to become financial free smart? And especially why would I do such a proposal to you? The answer is simple: because I am an entrepreneur who wants to share with you my experience and my life story which may inspire you and transform your own life. I know what means being poor. It happened to me to have nothing in my pocket, resulting borrowing from others to survive when I was just fifteen years old with the lost of our home as I said at the beginning. Graduate with a degree in insurance, I have always been told about the 'apparent life success for those with diplomas' but this was not the case for me. I had a short career in insurance business as a broker in 1994. The more I worked the more I was asked to double my targets. The more I earned, the more I spent in government taxes and bills and the more I became slave to the company. Two years later I travelled to study in Switzerland, then another degree in study of development at Graduate Institute of International and development Studies. During my studies in Switzerland I combined studies with full time work earning about £2300 a month enough, for a student to supplement the meagre income of student life.

While I was in England finding a new opportunity due to the advent of internet business, my little sister Helene from Neuchatel in Switzerland, whom I adore with all my heart, although my big sister that I follow directly and another little sister were living in Switzerland, I rather had trust in Helene, unfortunately she was abusing me. She was making withdrawals from my account without informing me, the one that I opened when I was student with her name as a joint account. Because I was still unmarried I did not want to leave at the mercy of the bankers all my hard work, if something should happen to me. She and I were so close; I could never imagine that it is my little sister who will empty my small saving. Living in London with my little cousin Louis Marie, a married young man with two children to support, I could not contribute to the expenses of the household. I felt ridiculous because it had been months since I could not withdraw money in cash machine. One day I took time to call the bank in front of my cousin to see what was happening in my account. Unfortunately, according to the last word of the banker, the account had been emptied of all its funds and closed down a year ago in Neuchatel. I felt betrayed by my little sister. How should I live without a penny, an unemployed man? It feels like a dream to me, I still could not believe what was happened to me. Why has she done that? Things did not work the way I was expecting, I found myself once again without a single penny. I could not stay longer with my cousin; I was a burden to him.

I move to Bedford to live with her little sister Solange a single mother unemployed, living in state benefits, with a minimum to feed his kid, not enough to add someone like me. But she managed to do her best as his brother did before, not to let me down. For those two persons, may god bless them, I still remember how kindly they were for me, thank, without them I would have been broken.

Having no penny to pay for any transport to quit, I went to Home Office and describe my situation, I was told "You'll need to get a job to treat, feed and clothe yourself, and I was then sent to the south coast. I was eating once a day a junk food I had never eaten before. This way of eating has caused me a gastric problem, and since that time I started to suffer from hemorrhoids. To my sister I wish her good health and long life, until God called her in the world of darkness. But I could not wish her success. Even god would condemn me, because she was violating the natural laws of universe.

Finding Job through Job Centre

Later on I started, finding job via a programme called New Deal in Cosham. A sort of bogus programme of government, whish is running by Job Centre. This is a place where Job Centre sends people, who have lost their jobs or seeking employment, to mix with people suffering mental distress, depressed people and people experiencing homelessness. This programme did not bring anything to my job search. I spent more time feel lost, stressed and anxious no solution for my Job research. Having spent nearly four months in that place, I did not learn something or find a single job by them, some people became even crazy.

The place in Cosham seemed rather conceived to park people suffering mental distress, drug addicts and long-term unemployed, who are useless to the community. During the time I spent in there, I wanted to understand the system, a bogus system that swallowed up the government funds and therefore the taxes payer. This New Deal is the same like Business Link another programme that was wasting time to small businesses and creative minded. The system does not work, except for those that are designed it to fill their pockets. In other words they were making money on the back of the government through this training course. The system as designed does not help people to find Job, but to create income for its creators.

I have conducted several surveys on beneficiaries of such programme during height years, this is the same song: a waste of time for job seeker. Let us read one testimony of the survey:

The Jobcentre's "NEW DEAL" programme is in my opinion, a form of punishment for the unemployed rather than a pathway to employment. If you have claimed Jobseekers Allowance (JSA) for less than six months, you are not required to go on a New Deal course. If you have been selected to go on New Deal course, you have every right to refuse.

However, to the best of my knowledge and that of everybody that I spoke to, no one got a job out of it. Nor was anyone on work placement after the so-called "NEW DEAL-COURSE". Not that many people are happy to do this rightfully so perhaps, because as a provider of any educational or work training you are responsible to enable the service users to make an informed choice about the Option they may be entering into. As demoralising and frustrating as NEW DEAL is, everybody who has been on it will testify that not just those looking for work that feels let down by jobcentres, the environment is equally appalling.

Whereby, users seat around doing nothing but to read newspapers that are over a week-old as their source of job search. In fact, research conducted by the Federation of Small Businesses (FSB) showed that less than one in five of its members were using Jobcentre Plus to recruit partly because the organisation is deemed to be failing its users.[1]

In 2006, having waste a year with Job Centre, I find a job through my personal research. I began working as production operator in a company named Cooper Vision. But I have never really worked with my university degree. I even turn down a job as a consultant with a salary of £33,000 a year, where I had to work from Monday to Saturday with one Saturday as a day off per month to work in factory, with a minimum wage, half of what I was earning whilst I was student in Switzerland. I really earn a good salary when I was student. In fact, it is the salary earned when I was student that I have set myself a goal. I did not want to earn money; I wanted to make myself a lot of money. Money is only an idea. If you want to make a lot of money simply change the way you think. Every self-made person started small with a dream, an idea and then turned it into something big. The same applies with investing. It takes only a small amount of pound to start and grow into something big.

That is why I choose to work in this factory to have enough time to build my own money-tree-machine before I quit the *Club45-45-45*. When I used to tell colleagues/friends that I do not want to earn money but make myself a lot of money, they would laugh at me. Hi guy shows us how! This black man is creasy! If you have your own 'money printer', what are you doing in the bottom ladder of the company? What does this entire story has to do with you? And so forth!

If you've ever been in a graveyard, you must have seen on the gravestones that there are small phrases and summaries of the life of people. I am sure you've never seen as a summary of someone's life, all his cars, jewellery, building and the amount of its assets in the bank.

Why? Because people will not judge your character based on material things that you had. Rather, what is important is what we bring to others, is what we do with our life. Those who deprive poor people to live better; can they take their wealth with them in the grave? Unfortunately, it has been given to human being to live only once, and it comes the time of the death. God had anticipated everything: the goods of this world belong to this world and the people arrive and leave as they came, that is without taking anything with them. *Give something to those that are in need, as a way of giving back to the community of a country where you live or the country you belong to.*

If you have the mentality that says: successful people are blessed by 'Gods' or luckier, then you're doomed. Instead, you might say: "Yes, this person has achieved it, and then I can too." I just have to model what he has done and what others have done by following their example. I am not a Pastor, a Preacher or an Imam nor Evangelist. They are the servants of wisdom, and they inspire us with what they know. Whether we believe in God or not, we all face the same life issues. I am here as an anonymous entrepreneur, there are plenty of opportunities like is never been before. I create my first business at age of 25. It closed down following the poor management of those who were in charge.

During that time, the Internet has started to grow and this was an opportunity to start a new kind of business. As I started at the beginning, this business model has nothing to do with financial advisers, financial experts or genius academic people coming from the Best School of Business.

Even the IMF or World Bank experts do not preach nor the word of Jesus neither that of Muhammad can guarantee us mistake-less service. They do not control our niche, most have never run a business and they are highest qualified employees. Why? Because, you know there are people out here who cannot read or write music, but are able to sing and interpret other people's songs. This means that you have the skills to achieve your dream in *Internet Time* by doing things in a simple manner. Why not be the next? You can be Internet Editor, Drop Shipping Seller, Coach Adviser and anything you want in the Internet Time. You do not need to be Richard Branson, Simon Cowell or some kind; you can make your own name. These young Internet entrepreneurs and others anonymous have proved it in the past.

Internet Editor

For instance, becoming an Editor on the Internet is the easiest thing in the world. When your objectives are clear and you are computer literate, it does not require enough money if you have good titles. E-books can easily be done in a corner of your living room on a PC or iMac. E-Books are selling like hotcakes especially with the growing up of iPad, Kindle, Sony Reader tablets. Finally, very few traditional publishers understood the revolution and the omnipresence of e-reading. They are still doing their daily routine of *hard-copy reading* and have failed to take into account the growing appetite for Internet usage. Just as music and film producers did not foresee the arrival of MP3, iPad, iTune and portable DVD players etc. However, some corporations such as Google and Microsoft understood this inevitable change. Likewise, I drafted this book at the time, these two corporations are currently in the process of spending millions of pound to scan all books that have expired copyright and are in the public domain, that fall under their hands. Amazon is equally, investing millions in electronic publishing. *Drop Shopping*, I will draw on this subject in greater details on another chapter.

Value of Information

Nowadays, information has become the single greatest asset. Not long ago, in order to become wealthy you will have to own or be part of a family that owns factories, oil wells, gold mine or cattle ranches. In this Golden Time, Internet can make you financial free smart. The young entrepreneurs who created You Tube and Facebook provide a great example of how vital information has become. With just a few thousand pounds, some information and the leverage of technology these young boys have become billionaires overnight. Poor information creates poor people in the Internet Time. Most people who are struggling financially are those who are using Industrial or Agrarian age information in what I termed "*The Internet Time*". For example, industrial age information could best be described, as ideas based solely on believe that, "I need a good education to get high-paying job". For agrarian age of information, owning a plot of land was the basis of or the only source of wealth. But if we look at how the world has changed so fare, the price of getting rich has gone down. Since the 1990s which saw the end of cold war, the advent of internet and globalisation, wealth is available, affordable and abundant for everyone with a little effort and good information regardless your age, your background, the colour of your skin or wherever you live. There are now about five categories of people: *the poor—the middle class—the super middle class—the rich, and the super-rich.* The Creators of You Tube, Facebook are an example of the Internet Time.

But there are still many anonymous people we don't know out here. Look around; the richest people did not get their wealth because of their educations. Look at Floyd Mayweather and Lionel Messi. Even Mark Zuckerberg, who dropped out of Harvard, co-founded facebook; he is now a youngest billionaire in the world. According to Dally New, there is a Football Club Anzhi Makhachkala on 23 August 2011, who reached an agreement with Internazionale FC to sign Samuel Eto'o Fils in a three-year deal that made him the world's highest paid player, with a salary of €20 million after tax per season. Can you imagine a black African earning as much as that?

Now here is a question: have you ever here of Sébastien consultant in marketing strategy nickname "Le Marketeur Frannçais", or Cédric Annicette of blog Forme Attitude; many not. Many of you reading this book never heard of me either. You see, there are tens of thousands of us out there, and often people do not discover us until they have a problem they need to fix. Cannot attract the customer? You find Sébastien; if you need to loose weight download the free guide « 8 recettes brûleuses de graisses » on Forme Attitude of Cédric. Don't know *who, what, when, where, how and why*? To start a business out there, you stumble upon Jean Drop-shipping Expert. Nowadays, Small Businesses are desperate for new customers and Consumers are using Internet more than over to find local products and services. Small business owners are not marketers; they don't know how to attract customers.

On Internet Business, storytelling are extremely very important, because the stories are viral, they capture the attention. Today, the biggest challenge is to capture people's attention to buy from you, and storytelling gives you a capital of compassion and a link to your list, they make people act, and we remember their message. Businesses, governments, politicians and all leaders use storytelling. When our brain has a list of point or things, it puts in the trash most of the things we have and keep only the stories and images. It is not a coincidence that the "people magazine" sold millions of copies, because in each of us there is a bit of 'voyeur spirit', we want to know a little bit the live of others. We attach to people not only because they are strong, but also because of their weaknesses. This is the way of an anonymous expert world, as it has been said; when the student is ready the teacher will appear.

I've remember, when I was employee in my workplace I have heard people saying: I'm not interested in money, at the same time you see them working 70 hours a week. Whether you are rich or poor, smart or not smart, happy or unhappy, money remains the most important thing to have because we all use it. We have all heard others at one point claiming that money is not the most important thing in life, but money does affect everything that is important. Money affects our standard of living, education and health. Statistics of

UNDP Agency clearly demonstrates that poor people have poorer health, poorer education and a shorter lifespan. So if you were financial free, you would be glad that you have enough money when you retire, you have enough money and insurance to care for whatever medical problem you might face. Stop worrying about working hard as slave for money, and wake up in the middle of night terrified about paying bills. Stop worrying about the fact that, one salary is no longer enough today to get by. Stop worrying about not having enough for holidays. Join the Club45-45-45 and work hard for money expecting that money will bring you things that will make you happy is also awful.

By reading this book, it will give you an opportunity to start your own business if you apply the method provided and follow the processes and the procedures step-by-step. It is simple but not easy, building a business requires a lot of work and pain, but will also give you great joy. Put yourself into coursework and it will certainly lead you on the pathway to financial freedom. This is also your opportunity to create the chance to win your financial freedom. As I have always said: "*I deserved what I earn, I created my own luck, and this is the result of my hard work, what are you waiting to get started*"?

We often hear that if you have money, then you must be suffering in other aspects of life. It is a myth that was created around money. Money is something neutral; you can have money, family, friends and leisure time, you can be happy or unhappy. Everything depends on how people manage their lives and their business. In fact, the money does not talk; it is a heap of coins or paper notes that can be treated as a pile of garbage. The issue of money is in our minds and not in money. Imagine at the moment you have finished reading this book and you want to start your own business straight away. As a result of the new ideas that you have set up, you decided to check your bank account for current balance and you discover that your account has been credited with an amount of £99,999; what will be your reaction? The answer is in your hands.

The message here is that money is not going to speak to you. Rather, it is your emotional state, your behaviour or psychological condition that will dictate what to do. The money here is not a problem; it is you who is the problem. I have met people who claimed that they are not interested in money and yet, they will work 70 hours a week in order to supplement their meagre income. When they receive their pay slips, they exclaimed! Oh if one could increase my salary for at least another £200, I would be better off. And when I ask them, do you live or do you survive? Some of them will reply that "I'm doing this for my children and then I will stop working". I often follow up with questions such as, and your children will do that for whom? How much money do you put aside for your children? When are you going to live what you love? Have you ever met a dead person who has advised you not to live well on this planet because there is a better life where he or she is living? Not surprisingly, I am still waiting the answer of this question, if you have one please let me know!

The reality is that we live in a world full of hypocrites. We are often hypocritical toward people that we do not even know or have any form of acquaintance. Why do rich people live amongst poor without any consciences despite the enormous opportunities that exist? Open your eyes and keep it simple stupid, it is not so hard. Do not be a blocker of your own success because the key to realising your financial freedom is in your hands. As the saying goes "Work is the prayer of slaves, the prayer is the work of free men." Twenty (20) years ago, most of those who seemed to be rich, those in suite, walking quickly in public transport, those who have big cars, business leaders were not accessible and did not seem to have time for poor people. Not even had time to explain how to create wealth. But with the advent of the Internet, we have many opportunities: books and information (paid or free). It is in books and on the Internet that we must be addressed our obstacles to financial freedom. From anywhere you can launch into the sky! May we via the Internet Business, launch ourselves into the sky of our financial freedom, from our creativity force?

This are some of the books that helped to enhance my entrepreneurial knowledge as well as the acquaintance with my first mentors: *How to make friends* by Dale Carnegie— *Rich dad poor Dad, Before You Quit Your Job* by Robert Kiyosaki—*Think and Grow Rich* by Napoleon Hill, *the Millionaire Messenger, The Charge* by Brendon Burchard— *The eBay Business Handbook* by Robert Pugh and *The Lean Start-up* by Eric Ries, and many others that I cannot mention for reasons of space. It is therefore, possible to be financially independent by following simple concepts. Asset creation has nothing to do with the colour of your skin, the neighbourhood where you grew up, religion, or the size of the legacy that we can dream of having on this internet time. On one of my website www.creer-pour-reussir.com, I demonstrated a simple method to create passive income; the hypothesis and analysis are based on a system that is saying if:

➢   55% of revenues are used to our daily needs,
➢   25% of our desires and leisure
➢   20% are invested in a project.

The remaining 20% invested will create income that will do the same cycle, and this will have a snowball effect. Why should we settle for only 15% of our income on food if we love the restaurants? Why should we tighten our belt with only 5% of our revenues for cloths if we like to look smart and if our passion is travelling? Why do we have to work extra hours and still complain about unpaid bills? When are you going to Live What You Love? With this system you are sure to make the most each month to save part of your income, in order to have capital to invest when the opportunity comes to you. I am not talking about *chances*, but of *opportunities*. Good luck! I am certainly not hoping for, I do believe in opportunities, we have examples everywhere. Just look at these entrepreneurs who made their fortunes on the Internet. Is it luck? NO! You can also see this opportunity on the Reality TV Shows is it another LUCK? NO! Young or old, previously unknown artists are now emerging as one of the best in what they do not by luck, but because they seized the opportunity that was offered to them by creating their own "luck" to succeed. They have used the opportunity that was offered to them and most of these artists may be young, but you can also do it at your level.

The only lucky ones are their children who will inherit the vast amount of money resulting in their financial freedom, due to the hard work and accomplishment of their parents. This is the chance to be offer your children the live that you never had, enjoyment without effort. If you win lottery, you must count yourself as one of the luckiest person on earth. But if you work hard and build your own wealth, you are not a lucky person because you have created your own luck 'it is as simple as that'.

The lesson is that, we must create our own "luck" seizing the opportunities that are available to us. The chance!! It will not come out of nowhere, you must provoke it yourself, and Internet offers tons of opportunities. You quite simply, can stop worrying about anything that money can take care of because it will no longer be a problem. Certainly, you will be living the life that you love when you apply *"The Jean secret formula to get ahead"*. I can assure you that this book will significantly enhance your business mentality.

Do you have these six qualities of the 20 golden secrets of business attitudes to succeed?

1—Do you like reading?

If you prefer to ask for directions rather than read the signs; if the last time you opened a book was in school, if you read this far and find that my text is an unbearable effort, you may find it more difficult to succeed, at least in one of the activities that I have outlined above

2—Do you know how to count?

If you do not like the numbers, I do not recommend you to embark on an online business. I saw one of my relative went bankrupt and end his life slowly because he confused turnover with profits.

3—Do you know how to use computer?

Are you familiar with basic computer usage? Typing a text in Word, install a programme on a computer, to copy and paste, I do not know the html, I do not want to learn php or perl, and I will show you how to succeed without being an IT expert.

4—Do you know how to spend Money?

If you are one of those who prefer to go to nightclubs, buy nice clothes, buy canes of beer and packets of cigarettes rather than a book or a training programme, if you are reluctant to spend £5 to win £50, forget it. One has nothing for nothing.

5—Are you curious?

Do you change your appearance each day or your surroundings? Do you want more than the others? Do you like to learn? If your dream is to be an employee, if you love the routine, if the daily grind is your personal drugs, then forget about the success on Internet business.

6—Do you have this character?

Smart people talk about ideas, Average people talk about events and dumb people talk about other people.

If you find yourself in the first character, the success on online business is close to you. So if you are ready to claim your part of wealth on Internet, learn *the remains golden secrets of business attitudes to succeed*. That is so simple, I did not say easy, but you can look behind my shoulders and copy the step-by-step secret system, process and procedure that I've followed to create the road to financial freedom as I did. I promised to pull back the curtains of my business and let the newbie right inside my years of hard works, something I am sure you will never see these big Internets marketing experts do. Why should I do this? To show people first hand how simple it is although not easy. You have to "be part of the game, not as spectator" and build a system for the financial freedom that never stops. Be aware! I did not say that if you want to become financial free you'd not work hard!! At least in early you have to work hard and hard, it takes time and dedication. Once you know how to build your own "Internet system for the financial freedom that never stops", you'll never have to worry about money again and quit the *Club45-45-45*.

Notice that, every successful enterprise, whether it's on Internet Business or Traditional Venture has an unmistakable secret formula. Why?

Because the natural laws that govern our universe are not done for some people, anyone who applies exactly the secret formula of success for a given enterprise can expect the same success that others have achieved by applying the secret formula. It is the same secret formula that Myspace had used before facebook. Then facebook came and applied the same formula by adding his own creativity. That is why the Coca Cola Company has kept very secretly his formula so that others have no access to it.

It is the same reason that $(1*10a)+5a+5=(10a*1)+5+5a=15a+5=[5(3a+1)]$ because it's a formula that works wherever you are for everyone.

We are always talking about what to do to be successful, but we don't always talk about the behaviours that lead to failure. And part of becoming successful is eliminating the bad behaviours. Of course, if you don't know what those are, it's hard to get rid of them, right?

Behaviours that lead people to frustration, struggle and even failure on online Business

a) Not investing in lead generation.

A business in internet time without a mailing list isn't a business. Every business should have a strategy for capturing names, not just from people who have purchased your products or services, but for prospects as well. Each new name acquired is a "gateway" to new business, repeat business, and referrals you wouldn't otherwise have. You can create the greatest marketing campaign in the world, but if you don't have a list of prospects to send it to or are unwilling to spend money to build a list, you are dead in the water.

b) Investing too heavily in one strategy.

Very often I see business owners use only the Internet for all of their advertising. Even worse, is using just one Internet strategy, like only sending emails, or only using Pay Per Click to drive traffic to their site. This is an error. I admit I've even fallen into only using the Internet myself, but I guarantee you it's not a trap I will fall into again.

c) Not knowing who your target niche market is.

At Dan Kennedy's Mailbox Millionaire seminar, Dan said, "At least half of the battle is won via selection, not 'creative' message, copy, offer, etc." Mediocre marketing aimed at a very well selected target market will get superior results. However the best marketing message in the world aimed at a poorly selected target market will get you mediocre results at best. You can't expect to effectively craft a powerful marketing message to attract your ideal customer, client or patient, if you don't first have a very clear picture of who that person is. Clearly define whom it is you are catering to, first. Then craft your message.

d) Not knowing how to sell.

The most successful entrepreneurs I know are also master salespeople. If you don't know how to sell, you are going to continue to struggle. In fact, in Three Secrets to Succeed in Internet Christian Godefroy discusses the thing *you must never do* that incredibly 99% of all business owners do that creates a huge obstacle to selling. Once people remove their selling obstacles, not only do they see their profits soar, but they speed up the sale and stop competing for business too.

e) Not taking action.

The one thing you will hear over and over again from most successful owners, who have transformed their business, in what seems like overnight is to take massive action. You can think about getting financially free all day long, but unless you do something, customers are not going to magically appear and start giving you money. The reality is that, the people in action are the ones who are the wealthiest. Worry less about failure and just get moving.

f) Knowing the Secret of Internet Business

The first secret of success on the Internet is not facebook. This is not twitter or Bing, adwords or google and any gadgets that have been offer to you. No, the First Secret to Succeed on the Internet and few people know is an *email address*. Each year there are more than 275 millions people who open an email account. Approximately 2.9 billion people on our planet use email and every day 297 billion emails are sent. Email is the best vector to communicate, sell and make you known. We call it email copywriting

g) Not using storytelling

On Internet Business, storytelling are extremely very important, because the stories are viral, they capture the attention. Today, the biggest challenge is to capture people's attention to buy from you, and storytelling gives you a capital of sympathy and a link to your list, they make people act, and we remember their message.

Focus on eliminating these behaviours now; you will go a long way towards removing much of your frustration and struggle in your business. The most successful people I know are constantly investing both time and money in learning. I've heard people say, "Well you have to be rich so you can afford to go to seminars, hire coaches and buy products."

The truth is that a person is successful because they invested time and money in training, coaching, seminar and new skill before they had the money to invest. Can you imagine someone wanting to get hired and paid as a pilot without investing in the education and training necessary first? I remember struggling to buy Christian Godefroy "The Simple Way to Start Internet Marketing" program for £447 about 5 years ago. I can't imagine where my life would be today if I had not invested in that. You have an opportunity to get some amazing coaching and training at the create-to-succeed.co.uk. So you know where you need to start and where you need to be tomorrow.

What you do not need?

You do not need a lot of capital.

The magic of the Internet is that, you can start with very little and reinvest it progressively. And the next day you can have a free website that will be more effective than a multinational. Most business that you would like to start whether is a franchise; a shop or even an office import export requires ten of thousands of pounds. Here a PC or iMac an Internet connection and less than £3,000 are enough.

You do not need to be an educate person.

I met many people in seminar who are making real money on the Internet. One does not know HTML, PHP he knows just to install a programme that he downloads free on the Internet. To tell you the truth, without having done any studies you can put on your business cards *editor*, it will open you many doors. I will tell you now what he sells. He wrote a book on how to become a professional footballer at age of fourteen. But later on he changed the cover of his book with half naked women on. What do half naked women have to do with football? Practically nothing! But it is obviously eye-catching. And the sales of his books have doubled when he changed the cover to this new version. While the number of over qualified applicants is increasing Internet business is very open to people without qualification. Another advantage is that this sector does not need a loan from the banker or premiership footballer wage.

You do not need to be a crack in computer.

I know plenty of cracks in computers sciences. They are not rich and are happy to work for you for crumbs of what you earn.

You do not need to be young.

I started my Internet business at age forty. I had to learn everything by myself. I know young people who are relying on state benefits, when some grandmothers are doing well on the Internet business. I also know a young Indian who is making millions of pounds in London on the Internet; he charges his four days seminar more than £1000.

Of course, at the beginning it will be necessary to cut down on the TV programmes the holidays and entertainment outlets; it is the part of 20% you need to bring to fulfil *The 20 Golden Secrets of Business Attitudes to Succeed*. But with time, four or six hours a day will be enough and when you will earn five times more on the Internet than anywhere else, you can drop your current day job. If you compare the time that required for an Internet business to any job where you sell your time, the Internet is a godsend, you will be independent and will no longer have to answer to a boss.

What do you need then?

A Mentor:

Someone who serves as a role model and shows you the way, it is a guide, someone who has made all the mistakes before you, and who knows how to speak to you. I had several mentors, no need to physically meet a mentor. I never talked to Brendon Burchard before I met him three years later or Christian Godefroy. But I followed their teaching and applied. If you are like me, you have probably noticed this paradox. As an entrepreneur, you are ready to work very hard for your business to succeed. But on the other hand, it seems the harder you work the lesser the rewards and it is almost discouraging at times. I remember how hard this belief was to me when I started writing projects for my financial freedom. I still see myself sitting in this cold shared house in my tiny room in Portsmouth, in England broke because every pound I had was going to buy books, CD ROMs, Video training that promise you to get rich quick. I was writing on a small table that I pickup in from a public bin with the help of my friend's wife.

So when you start to create your business and launch a website, someone would tell you to make a blog, another would tell you to write an e-book. You select a product to differentiate yourself from other, you discover that 3 . . . 11, or 101 competitors had the same idea or have simply copy you. The more you grow, the more you train yourself, the more you feel that your primary goal is out of reach, that each answer you get raises 3 . . . 5 or 101 questions! Here is the problem, your time is priceless and you need a plan, step by step. Because without an action plan you will be dispersed, discourage and give up.

A Partner:

The high-tech companies that have succeeded were mostly created by a team of founders, and not by a single person. In most cases, one of the founders had more business attitude than others and he quickly took the leadership of the project—Wozniak vs Steve Jobs; Bill Gates vs Allen, etc—. Exceptions are rare and you'll immediately think of Mark Zuckerberg, the young co-founder of Facebook, which is still in the head. But he was not alone at the beginning, even though it remained the only public face of the company since its launch.

To create a business, you must carry countless tasks: technical, marketing and communication, commercial, legal, financial, etc. A single person is quickly overwhelmed. External resources can certainly accompany it but for some, it is critical to have internal structure. Finally, start a business is to create a collective body, is leading a team, but also develops the ability to listen and management. It all starts better when you start with two or three people. The founders can support each other. It also avoids entrapment syndrome in personal beliefs anchored too.

A Team*:*

The first quality of a start-up is his team before the business plan, the product and all the rest. The entire of success, result from the ability of the team. This is especially true since many successes are the result of frequent changes of direction, service or product. While you want to start a project, it is necessary to gather the early skills that are rarely found in one person. Besides implementation capacity and organisation, same technology requires several skills between product design and industrialisation. This is true in hardware, in software and in online services.

Chapter 5

HOW TO START SMART ONLINE BUSINESS

Seeing What Others Are Missing

If you are interested of starting a business, there are a lot of advices on Internet. For example, just Google search "How to start an auction business," you will get millions and millions of results. Everyone has something to say about how to start a business online, because millions of people like you and me have the same dream of financial freedom, dream of mansion, early retirement; they are also looking for information and new products, and Internet is regarded as an information highway.

But could you read millions of web pages of advices? Do you have enough of methods that promise you to become instantly rich, as the 19 secrets of getting rich quick? Unfortunately, it's the same story as many of us have experienced online, resulting in empty promises that end up nowhere. So if you know what you *want to be*, you will find *what to do*, no matter what people say. Independent report and government statistic point to the fact that E-commerce is getting bigger and bigger every year and this is a result of small home base Internet businesses. This is a good thing for you and me; there is money to be made, and plenty to go around.

In fact, do you know how to build ecommerce website and Internet storefront? Or what a Merchant Account is, or where is the starting point? Where can you go out and say: Hi! Guy this is the first thing to do in order to start online business? Yes there are a lot of companies out there who tell you they will help you set up your online business. Beware; we are living in what could rightfully be described as the 'World of Hypocrisy'. I spent many years researching on Internet and there are a lot of scam artists (fake business), who are hopping you do not know where to start. They will tell you that you don't have to know anything, all you have to do is just send them £75 or £100 with your domain name, they will handle everything, your bank account, supplying you with the products you will sell, and your entire online e-shop will be magically ready to start. That is why I have written this book, to help solve the problem of millions of those who want-to-be entrepreneurs and create jobs.

This new step-by-step workbook takes you by the hand and walks you through the simple process. It's not so dark if you open your eyes; drop shipping will allow you to sell many different products with no up front investment. This means that you are no required to pre-purchase any products before selling them! There is no expensive inventory or warehouse to maintain and you won't have to take time to package and mail the merchandise. You simply do the selling and the drop-shipper does all the rest for you simple that is it! *I say simple but not easy*!

Before you dream to start your own business ask yourself the following questions:

Do I really have the Desire? The Will? The Self-confidence?

By reading this book you will know if you qualify, otherwise this book is not for you, and you can stop it and rather looking for a job or keep your job.

Pass from the desire, the simple will and the self-confidence in idea, most people who want to start their own business are stuck at this level, which idea to set up my business! When you go through "The Jean secret formula to get ahead" you will notice that, every thing start by being 'Hunger' to succeed in the life.

To start a business there are certain things you need to do:

- Change your behaviour on how to manage your expenses.
- Think different—Think big no matter what people say about you.
- What kind of business do you want to start?
- Knowing the difference between what is: urgent; important; not urgent; not important.
- Able to live without a pay cheque or payslip.
- Entrepreneur does think of their asset, not for their salary.
- Ready to learn from others, and be creative.
- Do you want to start alone or find a business partner?
- Where can I find my business idea? Is there any demand for your business?
- Do market research and work out who your target customer will be.
- Write a small business plan to know where your journey starts and where is end up.

Some details will need to be updated as you complete the next few steps, or you might need to complete the next few steps before finishing your business plan. A business plan should be a live document not to big, updated regularly. Once you've done your business plan, make a project plan what you need to achieve by which (target) dates to get you through the next steps.

How can I finance my business?

Knowing that four in five businesses fail in their first year, I don't want you to use a solution like re-mortgages if you have one, I don't want to be pessimistic, but I do not want you to end up homeless if your business doesn't work out. If you do not have all of these things in place, now is always a good time to evaluate at the *how* and *why* you are doing business so you do not end up on a river with no paddles and no idea where you are going, or worse yet find yourself in a boat that just hit the rocks.

My proposal is to start an online home base business with £1500 to £3000. This will bring you some experience to test your ability to do business. You will find in my blog: www.create-to-succeed.co.uk how I started drop shipping with only £2000 then grew it with ten e-shop using Fulfilment By Amazon.

Don't Give Up Your Day Job Yet

Most of us would love to be our own bosses, owning an office or work from home, and be financially free to live the life we want to live. Whatever one decides, we will always face the fear. Indeed, the slightest change will cause an anxiety, the fear of failure. But we must start a new way of thinking. The only way to change is to act finally.

The Internet has made that dream possible. However, the path from quitting your day job to managing a business online, where there are no bosses, no need for suit, overall, boot, hat and no restriction on sick days is still a long way to go. Running a business is not like walking on the park and the rewards are uncertain. You need to be sure that you are going to be able to manage the business—which you have the skills and the commitment to make it work.

Successful entrepreneurs really know their own business or industry well, and this comes through direct work experience. It doesn't matter if you are a cleaner, a care worker or a bank manager—if you really know your trade, you should be able to get other people to deal with you, but don't think people would join you easily.

In this regard, if your business idea is related to your current job, use your time at work to build your business ideas without interfering on your job under penalty of gets fired.

If you are planning to set up a business in a different field; build up a network of relevant contacts and really research your opportunity, then do everything you can to level that field. Speak to members of family, contacts and friends or relatives. But be aware that, hypocrisy is the first quality of human beings, those who pretend to support you are the ones who sometimes do not want your success. I went through this situation with some of my family members. Be smart before you entrust to your entourage your intension to start a business. Some of them might present an obstacle to you, if you do not have at least 6-business attitudes as I said before. Carry out research, but you have to spread your wings far wider than a spreadsheet. There is no substitute for actually speaking to potential customers. Find out what they want, what they will pay for. If you can identify a gap in the market and a set of ready made customers you will be reward if you do it right.

Learn as much as you can by attaining business seminars, workshop to give you the confidence that you are on the right track, don't waste much time on forum there are lot of unsuccessful people there who will make you scared or who want you to fail even they don't know you. One of the best ways to do that is to start by testing your abilities and comfort level in a smaller risk environment.

Entrepreneurship is about solving the problems of society, not starting a business for one's own sake. That's the way to earn your financial freedom by serving the community. A good place to start is eBay, Amazon or set up Drop-shipping if you prefer an online business start-up. Entrepreneur is risk taker and you need to be able to withstand some rocky times, this is a best experimental time for you to become an entrepreneur. It is the place where I started my own businesses without spending a lot of money, after being robbed by some family members.

By experience we know that, everyone is eager to become a millionaire one day. As a result of these dreams, many people are playing lottery with the hope of winning millions and quit the conventional rat race of life or the Club45-45-45. The envy of one day living a millionaire's lifestyle is almost like a trigger for us to learn the secrets to making as much money as possible

Before I quit my job, I knew the real reasons why many employees do not become entrepreneurs. It is the fear of having no income; no bank statement and only a few people can operate for long without money. It's still a lot of hard work that requires marketing skills, discipline, and the ability to live without regular pay check, a downturn in the economy, or a product problem that is not under your control. But what is an entrepreneur? *An entrepreneur is not someone with Genial Idea; but an individual person who has more Business Attitudes and the ability to take a Risk and turn his idea or someone else into Business, by Creating a Product or Service with Premise, Staffs and make Profits.* Entrepreneurs are different, and one of these differences is the healthy and empowered to operate intelligently without money.

The lesson here is that: a successful business is created before there is a business, and do not give up your day job yet, your job is a starting block for you. Try before you quit your job, and test out your product, service or idea with real life customers. Use Internet and social network wisely for what it is good at getting instant feedback. The chances are your first idea may not quite hit the spot unless you are very lucky, but do not be afraid to learn, open your mind and listen to the market. When you know you are onto something you can really get on with it. The path from Want-to-be Entrepreneur does not have to be a hazardous one, and the real danger is to do nothing. To create a business, you must define its objectives. There's a difference between the dream and objectives, for example:

A *Dream* is a desire without any action plan i.e. I want a Lamborghini but none has appeared in my garage. While the *Objective* is a desire with a detailed action plan like to be financially free smart.

SMART

Specific:

Create a Website on eBay, to sell women's shoes and sex toys. Start drop shipping with a product supplier in a given Category. Try a kindle system from Amazon to write e-book.

Measurable:

Create a Legal structure, legalise your business, such as validated by an official document.

Achievable:

Use the resources and experience you have now such as this Book, you will find your way for success.

Realistic:

Is this project is compatible with my current working time? Identify your activities and occupations to sort out your real need. Who else can give you a hand as a mentor?

Time-Relate:

In how many months would you like to start your business?

Being an entrepreneur is incredibly rewarding, but it can be occasionally feel like a battle, especially on the mental side of things. This is the point that many first-time entrepreneurs decide to throw in the towel, you should hold out.

Where to Start and How to Start

Where to start?

As I said earlier, you must create your business before even you start on the ground and learn the Jean secret formula to get ahead on create-to-succeed.co.uk. Try to go on holiday or travelling somewhere new you never know. In a fresh new place, so many ideas that you have never thought of before can come drifting over to you! Also read a lot of books and blogs to be inspired by ideas that have already been thought of to come up with your own creativity.

Identify the sector in which you want to act and do research on the products you want to sell and identify different suppliers and compare their prices. Do not try to create a new product; if you are selling physical products perishable or durable goods, it is imperative to make sure that you have an investor ready to give you the amount of money you need. When I started my online store, I used other company's products (OCP); I bought products from home's base wholesalers and suppliers.

As a newbie forget to buy products outside of your country. There are many scammers, fakes wholesalers and middlemen outside ready to take your money and kill your business. I call them *financial predators*.

The Internet in loaded with so-called "suppliers", and everyone who has a wooden garage or toys figurines to sell wants you to think they are real live wholesale supplier. For instance, drop shipping agent or broker networks are often advertised as a drop shippers and bulk wholesalers even though this is not illegal, but they are not always what you think they are. They used the phrase like: *your wholesale supplier, direct to your shop and this is your road to Internet Millionaire. They claim that getting rich on the Internet is easy, do not let your chance of owning a real business to be ruined by them.* As you may have guessed, this golden book is all about how you can start your business and make money on Internet, by positioning and repackaging information that are in the public domain. It also and introduction to an in-depth practical-training-study I use in my blog www.create-to-succeed.co.uk. Developing this book is a project that has been on the corner of my brain for a long time. This book is a result of several years of research and survey that I have carried out before producing it. I even marketed a lot of information products with expired copyrights in the public domain making them available for all to use.

There are a lot of internet gurus out there who may try to sell you my training programme, or that kind of shortcut programme promising to make you an instant internet millionaire, but I warn you that will always lead you down to poverty. These so-called real estate gurus, stock-market expert; they have never made an honest income on the web. I'm not some professors or consultants who've never risked a penny of their own money in a business. Everywhere you turn they have the same story, virtual on every corner there is one.

The lesson here is that, use the verified trade portals even you have to pay certain fee such as, pay as you go or a membership fee etc. You might say why purchase information when you can get everything for free from Google search?

Well, let us set a little experiment and type for example "How to start a business on Internet", in Google. How many sites do we have to visit for all the information we need? 5-99 results; of course not, in fact, you are likely to end up with a result of over 2,320,000 on Google. Do you have the envy searching around 2,320,000 sites? I think not.

Indeed, if an expert takes time to analyse and digest everything by producing a well written and practical easy-to-read book, which sums up everything that is important on the subject, whatever the price, it will be cheaper than spending hundreds of hours on Google search for information about starting up an internet business. In other words, consuming thousands of hours of your precious time reading up these 2,320,000 web pages is very challenging. If you intend to sell information products you need to attend training seminars, learn how to make video, how to speak, even how to write e-book. As a newbie entrepreneur, you can buy from outlet or end of line products. There are thousands upon thousands of home base wholesalers and suppliers willing to sell to you if you approach them with well-written proposal or business plan. At the end of this book you will know where to get those suppliers and how to write the commercial letter easily.

How to Start?

There are hundreds of books, courses and websites on inventing and licensing products. But the problem is that the conventional wisdom is completely backward. In fact, several studies have shown that 98% of all new product ideas fail. For instance, the United States Patent and Trademark office issued 456,106 patents in 2009 with full reporting statistics. Yet, according to the U.S. Patent Office, only around 2% of those products ever made it to market. What is responsible for such dismal results? The conventional wisdom for developing products and taking them to market is backwards and it kills 98% of great product ideas before they ever have a chance. But this will not be the case with your business if you employ this four; "create-to-succeed" process as it is completely different. Below are the four processes:

➢ Do not invent new products. Find a hot-selling product or service that is already being sold to a large market by large corporations.

➢ Improve that product by adding a new or different feature.

➢ Spend 90% of your effort on test marketing your improved product, not on patenting.

➢ License your new version of the product to one of the large corporations that already sell the old version.

In order to maintain the effectiveness of the four processes as outline above, it is advisable to collect an upfront fee (from the corporation you license your new version) as well as royalties for as many years as your product is sold. You will always make more money if you are creative and different. Remember, *Successful people have actually failed in several attempts than unsuccessful people. Because of their determination to have financial freedom, they became successful. They just keep on keeping on working on their dreams.*

The bottom line is that, you can go to www.create-to-succeed.co.uk and learn The Jean Secret Formula to Get Ahead. This is not a rocky science, it is just a common sense practice; the exact method I used to acquire my financial freedom. According to many researchers, a young person who finished his studies nowadays must exercise more than four different jobs in his life can you imagine that? Why? Because the world is moving at an astonishing speed! This is quite normal. We are in a golden age of information, the *Internet Time.*

There is a simple method that is growing at an unprecedented rate with every sign that it will grow even more in the future and I am still using the system to make more money.

A proven business model with one of the Internet largest companies in the world and this company is Amazon! How can you tap into one of the hottest markets on the Web? According to Amazon, by the time a customer buys one paper book, up to 1.8 % of e-Books are sold, that is, it sells almost twice as many e-books! E-books are in the process of changing the publishing industry, as we know it before. If you want a new challenge, rely on yourself, chase your dream, but live in the real world with your foot on the floor, even if you have lost your job, this is a good opportunity to move on with *Internet Time.*

Working towards your aims

Now that you're clear about your long-term aims we need to look at how you're going to get there. In order to succeed your aims need to be **SMART.** This stands for

- **S**pecific.
- **M**easurable.
- **A**chievable.
- **R**ealistic.
- **T**ime-related

Let's compare two examples of model aim

1—A Model That's Not a Smart Aim

Imagine that you dream of working in Dentist Surgery. This is not specific or measurable because we do not know exactly the type of work that you want to do in "Dentist Surgery". Your objective of working in a 'Dentist Surgery' is very vague because you have not clearly stated whether you want to become a dentist and running your own surgery business? This may well meant, working in a Dentist Surgery Practice as a secretary. How will we know when you have achieved your aim? The aim is not time-relate either. You have not said by when you want to be working in Dentist Surgery. It could be next month, next years or in three years' time. Therefore it's hard to say whether your aim is achievable or realistic.

2—A Model That's Smart

In other hand a smart aim would be: I want to take and pass the Dentist Technician exams by the beginning of next year. This is specific because we know exactly which assessment you are talking about. It's measurable too; we can see how well you are moving towards this goal and can tick off parts of the syllabus as you cover them. It's achievable; you have given yourself enough time to complete the course comfortably and still have plenty of time for your other commitments. It's realistic and time-scale.

Dealing with interruptions

Even when doing training, time has been scheduled in, it's quite common for daily activities to encroach on this time. Life often just gets in the way. The telephone rings, your child needs help, a friend pops around. Obviously you are facing a lot of distraction when you need concentration to achieve something and this can led to frustrations because your training is not getting the attention it deserves. It is much better to have a strategy to deal with this type of distraction and interruption that puts you back in control of your time. In this light, the strategy you need is simply to decide whether the task is *urgent or not, important or not*.

This diagram may help you to tackle the problem.

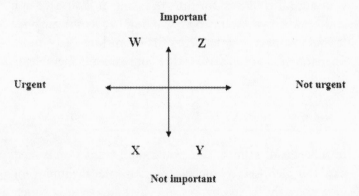

Tasks, which are *urgent* and *important* section **W**—These are tasks that you need to do yourself now. Example your daughter is in hospital you must pay the medicine for her treatment. As a result of your daughter's illness, you have a cheque that you need to pay into your account before taking care of her hospital bills otherwise you will go overdrawn and incur charges.

Urgent but unimportant tasks, in section **X**-Require your immediate attention, but do they really? Yes the phone is ringing but it may only be a cold caller, can you let the answer phone take it?

If something is urgent and important you need to give it attention, but make sure that you're no wasting time on unimportant tasks. Remember that a lot of section **X** activities can be given to someone else to do.

Tasks in section **Y** are *not urgent* and they are *not important*. This section has a lot of fun activities even we need it in our lives, and they can be time wasters. Example browsing the Internet, watching TV also fit here. Yes it might help relax, but won't you feel better to achieve you goal and be financial free in smart manner? Make sure that you're in control of your time, not just passively letting it slip through your fingers.

Section **Z** is the area that often gets overlooked. It's very easy for the urgent tasks and fun activities to take up all our time. That's why it's so important to stick to your time plan and keep an eye on your aim. You need to create your ***own urgency***.

Make sure that anything that interrupts, distract or delays your training sessions really is unavoidable. If not, put it off until later and give your course and aims the priority they deserve. That is the only shortcut in achieving financial freedom.

Choosing where to study

Some people like to study from the comfort of their own home, libraries or quiet room at their workplace. Nowadays, we need constant access to computers for various reasons i.e. training courses. If you have one at home (which I assume you do), try to set it up in a quiet area where you have some space to leave your book and notes. If others are listening to music or watching TV, try to work in a different room. If you're alone at home switch the answer phone on so that you won't be interrupted or disturbed by phone calls. Don't forget you can go to your local library. Make a mini-note on index cards, which you carry around with you in your pocket or bag. Whenever you have a little time to spare (while waiting in a queue for instance) you take them out quickly test yourself on the topics. It is amazing how useful those odd three minutes can be valuable.

Getting support from other

If you live with other people it will help enormously to have their support and understand while you are doing the training. They can provide encouragement and ensure that you have the space to do your homework without too many distractions. It's good to let your friends and relative know that your priorities might change slightly over the coming month. But be aware we are living in hypocrite world; there are *blockers, unsuccessful* people and *jealous people* who might want you to fail. The best way is to find a "mentor" someone who can help you to achieve your goal.

Memory

Our memories are amazing tools. They store vast quantities of information and keep a large proportion of it, as we grow old. To get the most from our memories though, we need to treat our memory with respect. This is especially important when you are learning a new subject. As an adult you do not have a lot of time to spare and you want every minute that you spend studying to count.

The first important thing to remember is to take regular breaks during study session. Do not sit down to a long session and keep going without any breaks for several hours, this is not actually a very efficient use of time because the amount of subject that we can recall tends to get progressively worse unless the mind is given proper rest.

Let's imagine that you have managed to clear six hours at the weekend to do some serious training. Your first approach would be to read through as much of the chapter as you can in those six hours and then say to yourself: ok, I've read half of the lesson! But how much of the subject would you remember at the end of those six hours?

A different approach would be to read a smaller amount but really make sure that you understand it and that it stays in your head. So rather than rushing on through all the chapter you stop every two hours so take ten minutes to recap what you've covered and have fifteen minutes break. Now, you might think that all this stopping and starting is a waste of time. But at the end of the six hours lesson you would remember and understand close 80% of the material. That's much more efficient!

As you know, we have both short-term and long-term memories. We use the short-term memory to remember things that we only need for few hours, such as where we left the car in the car park or what we must remember to buy for diner. We do not need to keep these things in our head for very long so there is no point in giving them long-term memory space. But when we are learning a new subject we want the information to stay with us longer even forever.

If you really want something to stay in your long-term memory, you need to keep testing yourself each time you sit down to study. The important aspect is training, before you begin on new subject, spent ten minutes recapping what you learnt in your last session. You will see that by revising information regularly, you can keep 90% of it in your memory, ready to use at any time.

As you work through this golden book, always keep your goals in mind and remember what you are trying to achieve (financial freedom). Do not be disheartened if you find some aspects of the training difficult and remember that nothing worth achieving is (100%) easy. Far, too many newbie entrepreneurs give up new projects at the first hurdle. In fact successful people however are always the ones who persevere regardless the obstacles that stand in their way. Your mentor, your tutorial as well as the support team are there to help; the rest is up to you.

What is the personal reason for starting a business?

As we begin this book of how to become an entrepreneur, we know that entrepreneurs are risk takers and they need to be able to withstand some rocky times, it is important to understand your own motivation for wanting to build a business. Ask yourself the following questions:

1- Why do I want to own my own business?
2- How hungers do I want to own my own business?
3- At what level do I want to play the game?
4- Am I willing to spend the time to learn about other successful entrepreneurs and their business?
5- Can I learn from my mistake?
6- Can I build a team, or do I like to work alone?
7- Do I need a pay check, or am I willing to reinvest in the business until the business succeeds?
8- Can I turn my fear of failing into a strength that will help me drive the business?

As you are answering these questions, if you are still determined to start a business, take it one step further and ask yourself the following questions:

o   What have been my greatest successes?
o   What have been my greatest failures?
o   How many times have I worked for free?
o   Am I willing to educate myself in all areas of the business?

What Problem does our business solve?

I have been studying this online business for the past seven years and have tried to understand why some companies have succeeded whilst others are struggling. For example Amazon was a mail-order-bookshop just faster and cheaper. Ten years later Amazon became famous by creating a great online bookshop. Today, Amazon is selling different types of products and has even expanded their brand by creating electronic books, which are selling more than paper books. According to Amazon, when one paper book is sold, up to 1.8% electronic books are sold. Another example is *eBay*; it consists of millions of people that together form a trading community consisting of individuals and businesses all using the eBay systems to trade millions of items every day. EBay, is an online market place that enables trade on a national and international basis and without the use of Internet, those companies could not exist. It is the Internet that gives them their power by allowing an audience of millions to share the services that they offer. However, those that have kept their traditional way of selling at the time these two companies were growing cannot compete with them today. This is just to illustrate that, it is not about selling in the old system, rather, it is about putting in place a *system or strategy* that works for your products as it is the case with Amazon and eBay. Like their success, we have also scrutinised the success of another company known as, *Cash Converter*. This company does not manufacture any product and yet, it is everywhere in mainland Europe simply by using other company's products (OCP) to make profit whilst many companies with good production facilities or factories are closing down or declaring bankruptcy.

Bearing in mind the success of what many will perceive as simple ideas, we questioned ourselves as to what lies beneath their success when other major companies closed down due to the global economic crisis. I am not saying this to roll some sort of mechanism or trying to impress you. This crisis was not cause by migrant workers such as; Polish, Indians Bangladeshis or shop workers. It was precipitated by international bankers, some of whom are close to home. It was the result of irresponsible banking on £1milion bonuses, not the industrious migrant workers on minimum wage who are to blame for this financial calamity. In this light, I came to a conclusion that it is because those behind these companies have put in place a '*powerful business system*' that works for their customers. They know for the most part what people want. In this regard, this perhaps highlight not only the influence of Internet, it also illustrate that if you are creative you can dramatically change your lifestyle without any loans pending on your head. These Internet billionaires have proved it. Is it Mark Elliot Zuckerberg who invented Internet? *Co-founded the social network, Facebook out of his college dorm room? He left Harvard after his sophomore year to concentrate on the website; the user base of which has grown to more than 700 million people, making him now a youngest billionaire in the world.*

We also know that: In any community there are people who want to do things, which have a passion, based on an idea, a skill, a hobby or an interest that they could turn into a business. All they need is a little help, someone to break down the barriers to success. If no one is prepared to take a risk with those who do not have a good credit ratings, or track record of running a company, it is inevitable that we will loose the potential of creativity and talented individual's". Nowadays, online business has made it available for everyone who has ever dreamed owning his or her business without begging a banker for loan. If you want to change your lifestyle a little bit or make a complete transformation, this book is here to inspire you. The information contained here are things that happened to me, and everything I talk about in this book to do, I have already test in many business, and in our training programme. For instant How to create:

—*"A Million Pound Internet Business Plan turnover with a Capital of £3 Thousands and 3 People"*—

Virtual Business Plan

Starting a virtual business doesn't mean that your project should be "kept in your head?" If you haven't written a business plan yet, your business is still in the dream business. All entrepreneurs face the challenge of starting a new business venture. This can be an innovation finding the right opportunity to get into, or starting drop shipping. No matter what type of e-business you choose, it is going to fail if you think you can jump into the pool without getting your feet wet first by developing a good business plan. Very often, the first 30 percent of the time that you will spend developing complete plan will save you 70 percent of the time later in achieving the business goals you've set.

One of the big mistakes that newbie entrepreneurs often make is thinking that Internet Business not being a *Real Business*. Another mistakes you can make as a newbie is not to sit down and figure out how much your business will cost you to set up, how much it will cost you per day to maintain, how much money you can expect to make in a day, and how you expect to expand the business exponentially so that it becomes a site that is a money-tree-machine.

A *Total-Money-Tree-Machine-Business* is a site that "keeps making money for you because it is well set up, functional, and what it sells never goes stale in the eyes of the public." It brings you ongoing, ever increasing amounts of income as time goes on.

Many people avoid writing a plan; I think for the same reason students don't do their coursework. It seems like too much works, and the reward isn't immediate and apparent. Many newbie entrepreneurs drag their feet when it comes to preparing a written document. They argue that their marketplace changes too fast for a business plan to be useful or that they just don't have enough time to create one. Even though time may be of the essence, it is a huge mistake to think that you can build the foundations of your project without a map. If you're frustrated by the thought of a length and complex process, don't be. It's not so hard. It's as simple as answering the standard *who, what, when, where, how and why?* Combine those answers with some goals for your project and an organised task list and you've got a good basic plan.

The important thing here is not how good the plan look like, but how good is it. And the most important thing is you've got one! Remember that you are not necessarily creating a business plan to promote yourself to others. You are primarily creating it for you so that you don't lose sight of your personal vision or goal. It is like a memo to you, so keep it fair and make it profitable.

The great news about the Internet is that you don't need to have any experience on the Internet at all, because there is always someone available who can provide the services you need. You don't need to have the technical skills to build the website; there are thousands of freelancers out there on websites such as esource.co.uk, rentacoder.com, guru.com and elance.com that would love to build a website for you at very low prices. You don't need to have marketing experience; there are thousands of marketing consultants that can help you doing things like improve your rankings in the search engines or pay-per-click advertising. You must develop the ability to delegate some tasks to the right person or the right functions even to servers and helpful software, so that you do not run the risk of burning out.

Chapter 6

WHAT IS DROP-SHIPPING?

Let's begin by reviewing the distribution chain as a way to understand how drop shipping fits as a business strategy and determining if it will work for you as a model.

A *drop-shipper* is a wholesaler who sells you a product and will ship the product to your customer. There are two kinds of drop shipping.

The **first type** is sometimes, referred to as manufacturing wholesale drop shipping. There is *a minimum quantity* requirement that you have to buy; if you do not sell the full minimum at once you end up with an inventory. This type of wholesale drop-shipping is usually referred to as "light bulk" wholesaling but you need to be aware of the minimum quantity requirements when doing a drop-shipping set up.

The **second type** of drop shipping that I am most interested is the wholesale drop-shipper who has *no minimum quantity*, and will ship to your customer directly. Often, the packaging has your company name; rarely will be identified as coming from the drop-shipper. Drop-shipping sometime, is thought of as a form of fulfilment, but here you do not own any of the product or inventory. Using a drop-shipper allows you to concentrate on selling your product rather than worrying about stock, packaging, or delivering. But you will want to make sure that everything gets sent out. If there are problems with shipments, the customer will be coming back to you and not to the wholesale drop-shipper. Affiliating with a wholesale drop-shipper enables you to work on product promotion, get profit from your effort and become successful.

In a **Traditional Distribution Chain**, you as the retailer purchase an inventory of products from manufacturer the creator of the product, wholesalers or distributors.

Wholesaler usually provides products to distributors; may sell directly to retail buyers.

Distributor purchases from manufacturers and wholesalers and works to distribute products to as widely as possible.

If you purchase from the manufacturer, you pay the manufacturer's wholesale price (MWP).

If you purchase from a wholesaler or distributor, you pay the MWP *plus the mark-up charged* by anyone else in the distribution chain.

Let's say for example, *you buy from a distributor who purchases from a wholesaler, and that the original manufacturer's wholesale price (MWP) was £10.00 /unit.*

Below is what you would pay in this case:

£10.00 (MWP) + wholesaler's mark-up of 10% (£1.00) + distributor mark-up of 10% (£1.10) + packing & posting (£ 0,50/unit) = £12.60/unit.

You maintain an inventory of the product, market and sell it to your customers at a market up price that will cover your costs of marketing, inventory and so on, for example, £20.00/unit. (£5.00 to cover your costs and £2.40 profit/unit)

You package and ship the product to your customer, charging your retail price plus the cost of packing and posting. £20 + £3.00 packing/posting, your profit is £2.40/unit.

In the **Drop Ship Model**, you arrange to sell products offered by selected manufacturers, wholesalers and/or distributors.

You do not purchase inventory. Instead, you promote the products through photos and information provided by the supplier and/or by showing sample products. Remember, Drop Ship has been around for decades it is not something new just since the e-commerce came along. There are standard practices in drop shipping that have been tested for many years, and Drop Ship Fee is one of them which are the *Handling* part of *Posting & packing*. It is important to understand exactly how it works. When a wholesale supplier drops ship one single item for you, they are doing a lot of extra work for you. You have to learn that your time cost your business money, if you can get someone to warehouse, package and ship your products for you, you are not only save all those expenses, you save time. Use that time to promote your business, instead of standing in your garage packing boxes.

For example, let's say your customer: Mrs Debora orders luxury handbag from your online website.

Your Store's Retail price for the Luxury handbag: ***£39.95***

Your Store calculates Shipping to Mrs Debora's door at £4.50

Your Distributor charges a drop ship fee of £2.00

*If you're charging the drop ship as handling Mrs Debora's Total will be £39.95 plus £6.5 Posting & Packing (P&P) or Shipping & Handling (S&H)=**£46.45** [4.50 Shipping plus 2.00 Handling (drop ship fee)]*

*If you're charging the drop ship fee as part of your price, then your Store's Retail price for the luxury handbag will be 39.95+**2** = **£41.95**, and Mrs Debora will only pay £4.5 in shipping & handling. Total: 41.95+4.5=**£46.45***

Remember drop ship fees are almost charged on a *per address* basis, but some drop shippers charge fee on a *per box basis* it's rare, but does happen sometimes.

How the process works

- You open an Internet Store, ecommerce or start an account on an auction site like eBay, Amazon.
- You find a Wholesale Supplier who is willing to Drop Ship the products you want to sell.
- You receive images and descriptions of products you want to sell from the Supplier and place them on your Internet website or Auction site.

- You promote the product on your website or auction site.
- You take the order, bank the payment and wait for it to clear.
- You contact the drop-shipper by email, phone or fax, giving them the item, customer name, and address— The drop-shipper invoices you with the agreed upon price.
- The drop-shipper delivers the item to the end customer, usually with your company name.

I hope that you will now have a better understanding of what is drop shipping. If you are just starting out in business, the inventory costs can be huge. Even if you are established, it may be difficult to afford expansion into a new line or stocking up in anticipation of the holiday buying season or the spring growing season. You don't need to purchase and manage inventory as in a traditional retail or reseller. Your inventories are paperclips, tacks and staples.

In fact wholesale drop shipping is really a good way to get high profit products without worries of inventory. Don't waste your time and your site space marketing products out of season. Ask your suppliers for a little historical information, regarding the best time to sell their products, everything is a season, and they have the figures.

Pricing your Products Of your work

Profit isn't just the difference between wholesale and retail, you have other cost to cover. Think about every penny you spend in order to get that product to the customer's door. For instant, your merchant account probably costs you about 3% plus 30 cents per transaction. On an item you'll sell for £20, that's 90 cents. Don't forget that calculation when pricing the item. Your supplier may charge a drop ship fee per item, or you may be buying boxes and labels for shipping wholesale products you bought in bulk. Remember to add that into your price.

This may seem very complicated, but it's really not. Just take the figures one at a time and you'll arrive at wholesale cost plus an amount that, when added together, becomes your cost of goods sold. Let take a drop shipped item that cost us £10 at wholesale, plus £1.50 drop ship fee, the actual cost price is £12.40 not only £10.00 why?

Product cost at wholesale: £10

Drop ship fee £1.5

Merchant account transaction fee for a £20 sale (20x3%) + 0.30) = £0.90. Total = £12.40

At £20 sale price, that product earns you a 0.38% profit [(1- (12.40/20) = 0.38

There is something to think about when you purchase products in bulk and ship them yourself. When you purchase a few cases of products from a bulk wholesaler, for example it's going to cost you a certain amount of money to have those cases shipped to your door.

If you purchase a bulk load of 300 products, and you pay £60 in shipping to get that bulk load delivered to you, you need to remember to add £0.20 to your cost figures for each of those 300 products. (£0.20x300 = £60)

Benefit

You only pay for the merchandise once you have sold it and collected the money from your customer Drop shipper ships the items you sold directly to your customer on your behalf

The shipment will not include their company name anywhere.

The shipment will not include the price you paid for the merchandise.

Your customers will stay your customers and will never know if a drop shipper exists

Your buyers will never know how much you paid for the products you sold

You will receive tracking information for each order so both you and your buyers can monitor the shipment of your orders

Drop shipper will handle all returns, RMA (return merchandise authorisation), or any other issues related to your orders.

Drop-shipper Problems

There are many drop-shipper pitfalls that you must be aware of as you start your online business with a wholesale drop-shipper. First remember that it is your reputation and not the drop-shipper's that is being seen by your customers. If you do not have a good relationship with your drop-shipper, you open yourself up to loosing business from your customers. Even the best wholesale drop-shipper will have out of stock problem. To avoid this drop-shipper problem, you need to do the extra work via checking the availability of stock of any items you are selling. If you are selling through your own website, are using eBay, or are using Amazon as your selling shop, you will want to check almost daily for the stocking levels so that you do not loose your customer due to this drop-shipper pitfall, especially the business which is going to be the life key of your Internet retailing.

Example of problem: If you are using auction, when you put up your drop-shipped item up for bid, there is a time factor until the item bidding is closed. Add to that, the time it takes for your buyer to get the money to you and you are setup for this stock out drop-shipper problem.

However, drop shipping is the easiest and usually the most economical way to start testing your ability to go into business.

As you set up your Internet retailing business, try to avoid the next drop-shipper pitfall such as: middleman and broker agent drop-shipper they are *financial predators*.

Over the years the Internet business is growing fast. Google search for drop-shipper or drop shipping and you will find millions of results. While many legitimate drop-shipper or wholesale sources can be found online, there are a huge number of sites developed specifically to scam sellers looking for a good deal. So how do you tell whether you are dealing with a real wholesale supplier or a scammer's drop-shipper?

The answer is not so easy, but there are a few things to check for that will reduce your chances of being the victim of a scam. While it is possible to Google to look for suppliers, that approach is hugely time-consuming and very likely to coming up with non-legitimate businesses. Save time by using the Internet more wisely. Begin by searching in a major international trading portal such as www.esource. co.uk. In addition to simplifying the search process; esource has gathered additional, important information about all manufacturers and wholesalers so that you will have an extra measure of confidence in working with suppliers. Be extra careful with portals that don't verify all their listings, as you could lose a lot more than there is to gain.

There are several different types of scammers around. Some are just after your cash; others are a bit cleverer. They actually do offer drop-ship services but the prices are just too high for you to make any money. These are not legitimate drop-shippers; they just use a drop-shipper themselves, don't stock anything on their own, and make on a profit in their transaction with you. Other scammers offer unbelievable cheap prices but they are away out of stock when you order. They are just after your membership fee.

If you do find a cheap source for big name brands, be careful that you are not falling for another type of scam-selling fakes. There are many suppliers in China and other countries selling fakes. They are legal drop-shippers, but just drop-ship fakes products. Any supplier that offers you both website and products to sell should be avoided at all costs. You'll end up with a website store that looks identically the same as everyone else's who bought one. Same exact pages, graphic and all the same products, only the names of the website stores are different.

It's like getting a thank you letter, from the Manager Director of your Company at the end off year for your hard work, or a thank you letter from the Prime Minister for supporting his political party during his election. We both know that the Boss is not going to sit down and type individual letters to hundred or thousands of his employees. Some secretary in human resource throws a big list of names into computer, and the computer prints out the same letters over and over again, each with different name:

Dear Mr. Juan Roberto P,

I would like to personally thank you for your hard work last year. Looking ahead, we are well aware of difficulties and challenges.

Nevertheless, we look to forward to a continuation this year of profitable growth, expanded opportunities and improved earnings.

Best regard

The Manager Director

- - - - - - - - - - - - - - - - - -

Dear Mrs Samantha,

I want to express my sincere appreciation to my senior executive colleagues and to all employees of the company for their achievement the past year. We have been fortunate to their commitment to 45-45-45 Internet Services and are determined to build upon it in future years.

We believe that the year ahead will be another strong year, one in which we will continue to build on past achievements and continue to generate growth in earnings and revenues. Dedicated people are the key to our success.

Sincerely yours

The President

- - - - - - - - - - - - - - - - - -

Dear Mr John Jonas Smith,

I would like to personally thank you for your support during my recent Election campaign.

Sincerely Yours

The Prime Minister

It's easy for them to create one website, and duplicate it thousands of times, one per customer. Then they take your money and plug in your Domain name, and they're done that is it! They make it look as easy as possible to you, and do not care if you ever sell a single product. This goes for eBay auctions too, folks. There are a lot of people out there selling overnight auction, packages that just don't work. You would see them online, in TV. Don't let it happen to you, it is too good to be true.

As I said before do not purchase any product out of your home base business if you are a newbie, and don't let too many hands in your pockets. Some of the greatest financial predators are people and organisation that we love trust, respect-people or organisations we think are on our side and are standing behind us. But the reason they stand behind us is because it is easier to get into our pockets from that position.

In fact, if your supplier only takes Pay Pal, Western Union or wire transfer is a sign of a scam; this may be a flag that the supplier is not a legitimate drop-shipper but a middleman, we call them the *financial predators* and they do not ask for your business registration number or your VAT number at all. If you have found a niche that you can consistently sell to and can absorb the costs of storage and handling, then you might be able to avoid the added costs of a drop-shipper by going to a light bulk or bulk purchasing situation to keep your stock supply. Drop-shipper actually can cut into your profit margin and you are better off getting your product from a manufacturer directly.

Anyway you are not Aldi, Asda, Tesco or Carrefour those, that can get huge discounts from manufacturers by getting large shipments at once.

Other Warning Signs

No or bad email address. Incomplete contact detail listed on the website. When you call, the telephone is on answer machine and tells you to leave a message, so they will get you later and the never call back. Your emails are not returned. Parts of the text or images on their site are copies from other websites.

How to recognise a scam

Being an entrepreneur is an Attitude or a Mentality. You have to change your attitude toward failure and I encourage you to read John Maxwell Book: *Failing Forward.* This golden book is not a university course; it is a *practical training study* to create a system for financial freedom smart. I do promise that when you will finish this book, you are going to have a very different view of what you can accomplish with Internet Business and what you have been missing out on. I think that when you see how simple it is, you will understand why I believe that anyone can duplicate this model. You can become a "smart" consultant and own your own local marketing agency as a part time or fulltime career that bring you respect, keep you sharp and could make you a fantastic income.

But it will not be easy if you go home and sit on the sofa, order canes of beer, bottles of vodka and invite your boyfriends or girlfriend, switch on your preferred channel and start watching Reality TV Shows that makes people rich!

Or go home and start watching a football match, when you have finished, then you're told that this player earn £120,000 per month and you have to go home knowing that you have nothing to give to your children, what happens for you who has seen the game? When you have finished drinking a beer in a pub watching a football game and in the morning you have no job, no prospect of having one, you go back to reality and you have to question yourself, who is to blame?

That will not work out if you lay on your sofa watching the late nights TV "The Home Internet Business in the Box" commercial information. The one that show you amazing systems that will make you thousands of pounds a week. They offer you Easy Step-by-Step Instructions with a little effort on your part. They want to sell you interactive DVDs, CDs ROMs that teach you ecommerce, without effort. They promise to reveal stunning secrets of pros that will make you rich with instant Websites and access to thousands of products that you can sell right now. Then they show you beautiful people around pools, swimming in crystal-clear waters in Monte Carlo, sitting under the palms trees in Dubai, while their businesses magically make them all the money, years and time it take us to afford those things. Common sense tells us it is not true. This has never been true. In our mind, we all know that there are plenty of quacks on the Internet and cyber-criminals taking advantage of our ignorance.

Let's talk about *scammers*: Scamming is when people con you out of your cash. There are hundreds different types of scams on the internet: fake loans with no upfront fee and easy monthly payment, fake lotteries and prize draws, work from home schemes, incredible schemes to make money quickly, fake investment; the list goes on and on. The people who run these scams are very clever and sophisticated and know how to persuade us to part with our cash I call those *"financial predators"*. Most cyber-criminals have some things in common they will:

➢ Catch you unawares, contacting you without you asking them to, by email, phone, and post or sometimes in person.
➢ Sound pleasant, well spoken and kind on the phone

or at your door and want you to think they are your friends.

➢ Have slick professional leaflets and letters, be persistent and persuasive, and rush you to make a decision.

➢ Even ask you to send money before you receive their tempting offer or the prize you won.

These quacks of Internet, from overseas and our country appear every day. They offer you something for nothing such as:

➢ The chance to join an investment scheme that will make you huge sums of money.

➢ A way to earn easy money by helping them gets untold millions out of their country.

➢ You have won a prize in an email draw by Microsoft for charity purpose or a lottery even if you have never entered one.

There are hundreds of examples but we can all protect ourselves by being sceptical. For example, is it possible that someone you do not know, will contacted you out of the blue would give you something for nothing? This is certainly never going to happen.

These scammers will ask you to:

➢ Send money upfront an administration fee, the list is endless but it's always a ruse to get your money.

➢ Give them your bank details; buy something to get your prize or other personal details.

➢ Not to tell anyone about the deal and reply only by email address they send to you.

They lie to you and give you what seem to be good reasons why you should do what they are saying. Do not send any money or give personal details to anyone until you have checked them out and talk to a professional or to Office of Fair Trading. If they ask you to do any of these things they are trying to cover their tracks and get your money and it is likely to be a cyber-criminal.

At Connecting Enterprise Ltd we have many years of research in this business and knowledge these people. We are good enough and we are constantly checking the works that are carried out on Internet business. However, in our heart we believe in hard work. It would not be easy if you do not do your homework or dedicate yourself. If not, your dreams for financial freedom maybe far from you. At create-to-succeed. co.uk, training programme, we know it is tough to start a new business venture, in this industry or any other. I like to tell those who want to start any business to prepare on the fact that, the first year in any business is risky, scary and frustrating. I am sharing this experience because I have faced that situation. It is always the first year that stop newbie in most businesses. They start out excited to follow their dreams of financial freedom and when the results come slowly or not at all, they give up their vision. They stop when their vision is not immediately matched by their bank account. It is easy to stop and have fun in life when you are not earning income at the rate and level you had hoped for.

The lesson here is that: Do not give up your vision or have fun because you are starting out a new business. Everything starts with *hunger to succeed in life*. Being an entrepreneur is an attitude, a mentality, if you let your own light shine; you unconsciously give other people the opportunity to do the same. As you are liberated from your own fears, your presence automatically liberates others. With an activity that thrives, you become a different person, a role model for your community. Have you ever heard about gymnast-cum-strictly? Whilst his method of conveying it may leave something to be desired, the message inked on Star Louis Smith's back is commendable. "What I earn I deserve it." In other words, you make your own "luck" via: focus, preparation, promotion and hard work. Wise words; let's hope that any young person who might otherwise go off the rails will take them on board.

Creating An Online Business

There are many different online businesses that you can create and here we are going to look at a two different types.

The first kind of business that you can create when creating an online business would be a website which serves a particular niche in the market. Many people have worked with this and this is often done by trying to find an under served niche, building a website, and then profiting of this small but profitable niche.

When you're building a website, you're going to want to find cheap keywords that you can use to help build your business as well as create good content. By creating the content and then creating back links between yourself and other websites, you'll be setting yourself up to have a high page rank with Google. By using Adwords to bring traffic to your website and then also developing your natural search engine traffic through building up a website, you will have built yourself a very solid business. If you are going to build your own site, you will need a web host that has at least ecommerce capabilities. The one we recommend since it is very complete in its plan and reasonable in its price esource. co.uk. They (as many others) include credit toward Adwords advertising. This is just one way of creating online business.

Chapter 7

CREATE LEGAL STRUCTURE

Introduction

We will consider the types of companies that entrepreneurs may start, explain the step-by-step process of creating a single member private limited company, as well as examine various services that can be used to facilitate its creation. We will talk about the various types of limited companies the basic legal requirements and the advantages of each.

The course will show you the process of registering your single member private limited company with Companies House, the government agency that regulates and oversees all such businesses.

We'll describe the documents you'll need to create and explain the content of each. You'll also receive an overview of the filing process.

The last part of our book will explain the various types of service providers that offer registration assistance. We'll consider the advantages of contracting for a ready-made company, using a provider to help you form your own company from scratch.

What is a Single Member Company?

A single member company is one in which there is one director, usually the owner of the company. That person controls all aspects of the company.

In order to create a company, you must register it with Companies House if you base in UK, which has a website located at www.companieshouse.gov.uk. Utilising this course will help expedite your interaction with Companies House and shorten your application time. We also help you bypass company formation intermediaries that charge you a fee to setup your company.

If you cannot do the formation of your company by yourself due to paper work, or a lot of reading and writing, it is better to use the company formation that charge you a fee and pay it; their services are useful. If you are base out of UK go to your Chamber of commerce to get the right information.

The Importance of Registration

Creating a single member private limited company through incorporation offers many advantages.

Limit your liability.
Provide you with a unique presence.
Establish your company as a viable entity.
Help establish your trademark and brand.
Authenticate your business as a legal entity.

Connect you with Wholesaler and Suppliers.
Create a consistent presence amongst potential clients.
Help you create an internal organisational structure.
Authenticate your Business as a legal structure.
Show that your Company has a legal certificate.

Incorporating your business with Companies House automatically helps validate your enterprise. It tells potential consumers and suppliers that you are serious about your business, by meeting government regulation, and looking to create a positive presence. Although the paperwork takes some time, it's well worth it. By limiting your liability, you are separating your own business finances from your private life. This offers you monetary protection if your company should wind-up. Registering with Companies House validates your company while providing essential protections to your company's name and presence.

The different types of Companies

There are four basic types of companies that entrepreneurs of small to medium businesses may form in the UK. Amongst the four, the single member private limited company offers the least expense, takes the shortest amount of time and carries the smallest financial risk. One on the four you may like to start is:

1—Private Company Limited by Shares:

Members of this type of company hold shares in the business. Because it is *private*, there is no public stock offering as with a public company. A private company limited by shares includes single member company's in which membership is limited to one person. That sole person is liable for the debts of the company.

2—**Private Company Limited by Guarantee**:

This is also a single member company; meaning membership is limited to one person. If the company fails, a member's legal responsibility is limited to the amount they guaranteed to give towards the company's assets.

3—**Limited Liability Partnership**:

This type of company, also known as a L.L.P, provides members with protections regarding financial liability, while offering them the structure of a traditional partnership. If the LLP fails, the company is liable for debts to the extent of its assets, but individual members and their private finances are protected.

4—**Private Unlimited Company**

In this kind of private company, there is no limit to the liability that a member carries. That means that there is more financial risk to the members. The amount of risk makes it less attractive to the small business owner.

The private limited company, whether limited by guarantee or shares, is the most popular type of business entity for an individual to form. Overall, it's fairly simple to create and run, allowing the entrepreneur to keep control of the company while engaging in a limited amount of risk.

Very attractive to start online business and drop shipping with the private limited company.

Private Limited Company Requirements

Companies House recognises that in a single member private limited company, the separation between the shareholder and the company is small, which could result in deterioration between the two and a compromising of the company's fiduciary integrity. Thus, there are specific legal regulations regarding such enterprises.

One of the most important aspects in safeguarding the financial reputation and security of a private limited company with a sole member is the keeping of written records via contracts, memorandum and minutes. In such a company, a single member may constitute a quorum and may hold a meeting and make decisions related to that company. Any meeting of this type must include written minutes and the creation of a written document relating to any decisions made.

Additionally, if the company contracts with the single member of that company for neither services, that are nor ordinary a part of the entity's normal offerings, and that same person is also the director, then the terms must be recorded in writing in a timely manner.

In UK Formation Law relating to private limited companies, there are no specific qualifications related to the office.

NB: while in the UK certain non-British nationals may be restricted regarding in which areas of work they want to operate.

Private Limited Company Officers

In order to be registered with Companies House every company must have officers who have been officially appointed.

Single member private limited companies are required to have at least one director.

Anyone may be the director of a company as long as:
They have not been legally banned from directorship.
They are capable of agreeing to the appointment.
They have not declared bankruptcy.
Age over 16 years old at the date of appointment.

Private Limited Company Office and Accounts

In the UK Formation Law, every company is required to have an office with a legal postal address that is registered with Companies House. Any official documents relating to the company sent by Companies House, Inland Revenue and other governmental entities will be sent to this office. The office does not need to be the primary business address. It may be the address of the company's lawyer, accounting firm or director. Use form (guidelines) to notify to Companies House of any change of address after your business is registered.

In setting up a company's accounts, it is essential that they start to be recorded on the day of registration. The initial fiscal year is ending on the anniversary date of incorporation; or on a date within seven days before of after that date. There are strict regulations regarding the filing of financial year information with the government. To help facilitate compliance, Companies House posts a form to the company's registered office with a reminder of the anniversary date or can be sending by email. There are automatic penalties relating to the late filing of yearly account information with Companies House and fines for private companies range from £150 to £1,000. Companies wishing to change their due date for accounting records may do so by filing Form (see guidelines) with the Registrar Account records are due:

- No later than 10 months after the end of the accounting period or fiscal year.
- In cases where the accounting period is greater than 12 months, no later than three months from the end of the accounting period or 22 months from the incorporation date, whichever is longer. Setting up a single member private limited company lets you retain control of your business with a limited liability. In order to register your company, there are different steps you will need to complete with Companies House.

Forming a Private Limited Company

In this section we will examine each step in the process of creating your own private limited company as required by the government agency Companies House. Creating private limited company has a lot of advantages, including limiting your fiscal liability and formalising your business as a legally recognised structure, while still allowing you to control your company. According to the Companies Act, one person may form a company or more for any legal purpose by adhering to its memorandum of association as filed with the government.

There are four documents that must be registered with Companies House in order to officially create a private limited company.

The documents are:

a. The Memorandum of Association Limited by share and Limited by guarantee.

b. Articles of Association Limited by share and Articles of Association Limited by Guarantee.

c. Application to register a company found at: http://www.companieshouse.gov.uk/forms/ formsContinuation.shtml#IN01

d. Additional information if your application includes a prescribed or sensitive word or expression. All forms to submit at Companies house can be found at: http://www. companieshouse.gov.uk/forms/formsContinuation. shtml.

These four documents comprise the legal outline of the company, stipulating various types of information, including the company's name, its directors and other members and the address of its registered office. These documents should all be submitted together.

1—Creating a Memorandum of Association

You can find instructions on how to fill the Memorandum of Association at:

http://www.companieshouse.gov.uk/about/gbhtml/gp1. shtml

To download the Memorandum of Association documents free, use the following two links: Limited by Share and Limited by Guarantee at www.create-to-succeed.co.uk

The details that must be included in a Memorandum of Association for a single member private limited company are:

The company's name, which must end with the term *Limited*.

The location of the company's registered office, to which all official correspondence will be sent.

The amount of share capital and its division into shares if any.

The limited liability of the members.

2—Creating Articles of Association

Normally these documents cost some amount of fee but you can download them free using the following links: www.create-to-succeed.co.uk. Articles of Association Limited by Shares and Articles of association Limited by Guarantee.

The articles of association delineate the internal mechanisms of the company. When creating a private limited company, you'll want to consider how many people will want to be involved. Many private companies include two people, both of whom have specific duties: the director and the secretary.

These articles tend to be more specific than the Memorandum of Association.

The Articles of Association include:

- The rules and duties relating to the director.
- The rules and duties relating to the secretary if you have one.
- Contact information for all members.
- How often general meetings will be held and for what purpose.
- The amount of indemnity that member has in carrying out company duties.
- The specific mechanism for shares, including how they are allotted, issued and repurchased.

You may include the director's duties in your articles. The director is usually responsible for the timely delivery of all documents as required by the Registrar including:

- Reporting on accounts.
- Annual returns form see guidelines (GL).
- Notices regarding the change of director form on GL
- Notice concerning a change of address for the registered office Form on GL.

The director carries out business on the behalf of the company and his/her duties should be described as such. The company is not obliged to hold an annual general meeting. The duties of the company secretary are not outline by Companies House, but they should include if you have one.

For all forms and documentation on these updates, please visit http://www.companieshouse.gov.uk/forms/formsOnline.shtml

Once this document is complete, it is very important that each member signs these articles and that the signature of a witness accompanies each member's signature.

3—Recording First Director

This form is to be completed in typescript or in bold black capitals. The form includes the names of the director and secretary, the company name in full and the location of the registered office. Once it's completed and signed it may be submitted electronically or mailed with all of the other paperwork. http://www.companieshouse.gov.uk/about/pdf/gba1.pdf

Application to Register a Company

This form is designed to officially register the company and must be signed by the director, secretary or a solicitor engaged in the formation of the company. It includes the name of the company, an attestation that regulations regarding the formation of the company are being adhered to and a request for contact information. This form is to be completed in typescript or in bold black capitals. http://www.companieshouse.gov.uk/forms/formsContinuation.shtml#IN01

NB: If the director is not signing this document, it should be made clear the status of the person who is signing and their connection to the company. This form should not be signed until the three other documents are written and filled out; because it attests that you have completed all of the other documents.

These four documents may all be delivered to the Registrar either via electronic submission or post. To the standard cost for filing by post or those who file using the Software Service for premium same-day registration, full details are available at: http://www.companieshouse.gov.uk/toolsToHelp/fileInformation.shtml

4—Company Names

Before registering, it's best to determine if the company name you've chosen is available. A name does not have to be identical to be deemed already registered. If the name is so similar that it would create confusion, the name would be rejected. Trademarks follow the same rule.

You are restricted from using:

- The same name as a company that is already registered with the government.
- Names that may be considered offensive.
- Words that mislead the public in terms of indicating a particular function, specific status or your company's pre-eminence as an entity.

NB: Any limited company's name must end with the word *Limited* (Ltd). For more information regarding how to search the Trade Mark Register, you may contact the Trade Marks Registry of the Patent Office at:

Email: enquiries@patent.gov.uk. Website: www.patent.gov.uk

To search for already registered company names go to:

<u>h t t p : / / w c k 2 . c o m p a n i e s h o u s e . g o v . u k /</u>
<u>wcframe?name=accessCompanyInfo</u>

Once your company is registering and its name incorporated you must clearly display your company name on:

All company buildings and offices. All letter head and electronics documents. All invoices, bills of sale, order forms, promissory notes, endorsements, bills of parcels, letters of credit, etc. All company websites Also, all business letters and order forms using any media, including hard copy and electronic, must list the company's place of registration, its registration number and the address of your registered office. Incorporating your business as a private limited company and registering its name is a useful process, limiting your financial liability, providing you with certain government safeguards and ensuring that your name is unique and protected. It also involves the annual filing of documents, adherence to government rules and regulations and keeping company information up-to-date with Companies House, Inland Revenue and other agencies.

You can register your company yourself using the instructions provided above, or hire someone to do it for you. If your company does not trade, your company is a *dormant company* and you have to pay a small fee every year to Company houses to keep your mane in their registrar.

Company Formation Services

In this part of course on creating private limited company, we explained the step-by-step process involved in registering a single private limited company on a basis of: *do-it-yourself*. Many entrepreneurs successfully, setting up their company on their own, by filing the paperwork themselves with Companies House.

But, if you feel that you're not ready to deal with paperwork as I said before, there are many online services devoted to do most of the work for the businessperson who is too busy for or simply confused by the overall process and various forms, jargons and searches needed to successfully incorporate as a private limited company.

There are two basic types of company formation services available. Some online providers specialise in selling ready-made companies that already exist and others offer all of the support you'll require to facilitate the paperwork to create your own company from scratch. Let look at both the prospect of purchasing a ready-made limited company and of establishing your own private limited company using an intermediary.

Ready-Made Companies

Advantages: Most of the paperwork is already done; you simply need to add a new director and secretary. This means that the application and approval process is often quicker than that involved in incorporating a new company. Additionally, a ready-made company has a history, which may give it more credence. When you purchase such an entity, it usually comes with the certification that there are no liabilities attached. Some ready-made companies already have bank accounts. Fees for such companies are normally half the fees of setting up a company from the start.

Disadvantages: The problem is that purchasing this type of company is seen, as the name of the company may not be what you are looking for. It is a way to get out of the gate quickly and be up and running in an instant. Does the story of the company have anything that connects you with your creativity?

Formation Services

Companies providing formation services perform a similar function as those that offer ready-made entities. The major differences between creating your own company from scratch and purchasing a company off the shelf has to do with the additional paperwork involved in forming your own private limited company and the need to create a unique name for your company. You can get basic services that include all necessary paperwork, name search and online filing. Prices vary depending what types or services you would like. To decide whether or not, you should use a provider who will provide you with formation services take some time to review this course and checkout the Companies House website.

Whether you carry on yourself of such a service or decide to create all of the necessary documents and do all of the filing yourself, you must first have a solid business plan that you will be able to facilitate your work and do a small online search for prices comparisons. Failing to do so will waste you a lot of time.

Additional Support

This is the basic paperwork that should be provided by any service offering private limited company formation:

1. The Memorandum of Association.
2. Articles of Association.
3. Recording First Director.
4. Application Form to Register a Company

Additional services that you may, or may not, need include, the price depending to the services provider:

- Nominee Directors
- Nominee Shareholders
- Registered Office
- Maintenance of Statutory Registers and Filing of Annual Returns
- Preparation of Special Resolutions
- Bank Introductions from £250.00
- Completion and Filing of Annual Returns

Many companies also offer:

- Secretarial support—Post office boxes.
- Telephone answering—Audits.
- Bookkeeping and periodic financial reports.
- Power of attorney—VAT Services.
- Telephone number—Company seal.
- Domain name—Laminated copies of documents.

Finding an online service that will provide what you need at a reasonable price will take time. But don't buy services because you are in a panic; always take some time to shop around and read all of the literature carefully and don't make hasty choices to spend more money than you needed. Often, because the interest of these companies is on doing everything quickly, potential customers will impulsively make decisions to purchase services that they don't need or may not use at all.

When considering these companies take at least a week or two to evaluate the value of what they offer. Do an online search regarding a company in which you are interested. Take some time to be an educated consumer or check with other business owners to see what providers they may like.

Expectation from a Formation Service

A good online service will do the following:

Offer advice and information regarding what you require to incorporate.

Complete all documents in a timely and accurate fashion.

Provide quick turnaround on all documents.

Offer a basic service that will get you up and running at a reasonable price (around £40 plus government and legal fees, which will equal about £100)

Keep all work in-house, not jobbing out to other countries or providers.

Provide a specific contact person with whom you will work.

The fact is that you will perform the company name search for free using the <u>Companies House website</u>. The four forms that are required are simple to fill out, especially if you read through this program.

The Memorandum of Association is a fairly simple document and the Articles of Association can be adapted readily or used as is from the government website.

If you are creating your own private limited company, you will need to be organised, motivated and focused on specific goals. Anyone possessing these attributes should be able to register their own company.

The service providers involved in self-made companies and forming new companies are useful if you don't have a lot of time because you are so busy creating product for a successful enterprise. However, do not look for these service providers to give you the secret to success. Your success will be based on your own business attitude and mentality, your drive and your ability to adapt to the ever-changing business landscape.

Whether you use an online service or create your single member private limited company yourself, it's clear that you'll receive various benefits, including personal financial protection, legal status and government validation as an entity permitted to engage in business. Not being yourself a member of the training programme, create-to-succeed, and as you do not have enough time to learn and implement the course, in addition to your business, it is best to hire temporal someone who has this skill.

I really want to emphasize this point: if you do not have the time or expertise to develop your project, you have no right to let these excuses stop you!

There are so many options available to you:

Buy training for your employees, partners or relatives, who will be responsible for implementation. To partner with someone who understands technology better than you or entirely free of the technique and make fully with "shoestring"!

Chapter 8

SET YOUR WEB SITE

We have been through the fact that scam artists will cheat you to build your Internet web site store. Now, let's talk about your Internet web site Hosting.

There are two legitimates methods you can use to start your Internet business:

Internet Store—Ecommerce hosting Providers. There are two things you should be thinking when starting out on Internet: Money and Traffic. To earn money you need traffic and to get the traffic you need to spend money. In order to give your business maximum sales potential, be sure you consider and plan the following elements.

Internet Store:

Advantages: You can create one store or several stores, easily navigate through them and change your products and pricing, and it's all done by point and click. There is virtually no programming to learn. The store templates look very professional, which definitely helps our sales. The sales and customer tracking are good.

Disadvantage: The store can all identically look the same if you're not careful. With some provides, you can change background and text colours and arrange the pages a bit differently, but they all end up being very similar to each other

Ecommerce Web Site

Advantage: You have much more control over the way your site looks and work. It is the most use web site to Internet business. You can create your own unique look without being limited by a choice of just a few templates such as you would be in an internet store. With dynamic pages however, you only have to create one page for each main section of your website. Each main page will interact with your database to display, for example, products dynamically; an example of a dynamic product page is: http://www.oursite.com/product.php?productid=15.

The actual file name is product.php (the file product.php**?productid=15** is not a file, it's a file + instructions on what to display within that file). The value 15 corresponds to a product in your database. If I want to view product 59 on your site, I would then simply change the url tohttp://www.oursite.com/ product.php?productid=**59**. Product.php is still the file; the only difference now is that it is requesting the details of product 59 from your database.

Disadvantage: You need to rent a space in the server from an ecommerce hosting providers, and building your own storefront. If you are not programmer and web designer, you'll need some help from someone or a reputable company to do this for you.

No matter which way you go.

You want your potential customers to be able to *easily get around your web site and find what they want.* Your online store needs to show numerous items at once, while giving visitors the option to simply "click" and get more in-depth information on a product in which they are interested. Allow your customers the chance to browse and enjoy your product.

Depending upon what you are selling, offering various viewing angles of a product can be enticing. *People want to see what they are buying.* Items such as shoes, handbags and jewellery are much more appealing when seen from various angles. Set up your displays so that related products are included.

If a visitor can't read about your product because the typeface or photos are too small or faint, they will get frustrated and leave without purchasing anything from your website. With readability, you're considering *how easy it is to actually see your descriptions and instructions* and how crisp and clear your images are.

Use words to connect your products with your customers. *Products descriptions should be well written and interesting.* By providing basic information about your products, it's effective to let the visitor know what an item will do for them in term of benefits. Directions on ordering product return and exchange policies or customer service should be easy to read and understand. A no regional telephone number for customer service can help create confidence in your site and generate more sales.

If a customer has to go through three or five web pages before a sale is complete, they may just give up. One of the major selling points for any Internet business is the fact that shopping online makes life simpler.

Make the process of buying something as easy as possible. It should take no more than three clicks from one page to another to make a purchase. The software you choose for the purchasing process will determine how long it takes to buy something. Carefully research your options, making sure that you choose software that's simple to use but that still has sound security features. Paying attention to these five elements in italics will help in the success of your online store.

Registering Your Domain Name

What is a Domain Name?

This is a name you will use to build your website so that public can find you in search engine. If you are creating a new online company comes up with the company name, and before finalising it. See if it is available as a domain. If it's taken, then try to come up with another company name and search that as a domain. It's best if your company name and domain name are the same. The main thing that should be in a domain name is simplicity. Choose a domain name that is easy for people to remember.

Registering your domain name is relatively easy, inexpensive and prices vary, depending upon which registration service you choose. Registering your domain name for a longer period than one year will be beneficial to your future search engine rankings. The registration company's service is free instantaneous search to make sure no one else is using that domain. Within seconds of putting in your preferred domain name and clicking search, you'll be told if it is available and given the opportunity to register it. Or you can use http://www.whois.sc for more in-depth information on any domain.

Selecting a Hosting Company

Through an online search, you will find thousands of hosting companies from which you can choose. There is however one important element to consider: always try to select the provider closest to your country. Most domain registrars offer to be your web host.

When selecting a hosting package, be aware that you will need to choose either Linux hosting or Windows hosting. Linux hosting is generally cheaper, and is used for PHP—an open source programming language-based sites, whereas Windows hosting is used for ASP and .NET—both Microsoft proprietary programming languages-based sites. We recommend you opt for Linux hosting, because PHP programmers are generally less expensive. More advanced users will be aware that both PHP and NET are equally powerful programming languages and that neither will leave you short of options when thinking of expanding the functionalities of your e-commerce store. When you registered you'll have free SSL certificate; Google Adwords credits, email and online support and more. Large companies often have the most competitive rates and innumerable services.

What You Need

For the first time you lunch your web site, there is no need to purchase an expensive plan. You can always upgrade when you need more space and more services. Don't waste your money on features that you won't use.

Here are the basics that you'll require:

100 MB of disk space—2 to 3 GB of transfer per month—At least one e-mail account—E-mail forwarding accounts—E-Mail auto responders. E-Mail aliases. At least 1 database, 24/7 supports. Front-page support, if you're using Front page to build your site—Daily backup and 24/7 File Transfer Protocol (FTP) access. FTP is used to transfer data from one computer to another over the Net. You can also add this programme

Protection of e-mail from spam and viruses. Secure certificates that let clients know that you are protecting their information (known as SSL certificates: a good inexpensive SSL certificates provider. MySQL, which is an advanced database management system using Structured Query Language (SQL). Authenticated Simple Mail Transfer Protocol (SMTP), allowing you to access your e-mail anywhere in the world.

Search Engine Optimization

When you build Internet website, your number one concern is how I'm going to draw people to my website? How among the millions of Internet sites out there today? You will need to promote your website, no matter with method you use.

Google is by far the most popular search engine. *Search Engine Optimization* means that you place the words that you think people will use to find your website, in your pages in the proper places. If you sell sexy-toys, use the word Sex Toys often on your website. But the reality is much more than that Meta tags, keywords, jockeying for position with thousands of other webmasters who are trying for those same top listings that you are looking to reach, it's not all that easy, and it takes time and patience. If your store is not found in the first 10 top pages of internet search results on any given search engine, it means that you're in trouble. If you need help check around for companies that provide Search Engine Optimization at a reasonable price. They will do the work for you. But do not let them fool you with a statement like we submit to 999 search engines, there are only 3 or 4 search engines out there. So remember to ask if they guarantee your position on the keywords that you want.

Social Marketing

In today Internet business, you do have to do this even if you don't want to. Blog post, article writing, Twitter, You Tube, Facebook, MySpace, LinkdIn, Tweeter and more are things that we need. The search engines ranks your site based on combination of both SEO and something called Black links, what we develop when we do Social Marketing.

In Social Marketing, the idea is to create information about what you sell in such a way it doesn't look like a sales pitch. You're not alone in the market. For example you write something like this: "we have a new great skin care cream on sale, could you get it right now before it gone!"

is awful Social Marketing approach. Never use that sort of sale anyway.

Instead, you've write about a good daily regime of newly skin care that is proven to work. Teach your readers what they need to know about the skin care, without trying to pitch them on what you sell. Why? Because the idea behind the social marketing is to get people online to share the information you create with other people in the social places.

PPC Advertising

Pay Per Click, advertising is away of to get your website noticed faster in the search engines. For example, you go to Google and open a PPC account, a program calls Adwords and you can find it on: http://adwords.google.com. You create small text ads for your internet website, and then place a daily or monthly spending limit on how much you want to pay for your ads. When your spending limit is reached, the ads stop showing until you top up again. The reason this is called PPC, is because you are only charged for each appearance of your ad if someone actually clicks on it and goes to your website. But today PPC has turn into a huge business and only makes the owners themselves rich. The right way to approach PPC is to use the natural methods first: SEO and Social Marketing, and look which of the keywords used in those methods are working for you. You should not rush to use this PPC until you start make sales from natural methods. It can easily turn into a life-sucking money pit from which there is no escape. Then you can pay advertising out of your profits, not from your pocket.

Chapter 9

FINDING PRODUCTS TO SELL

What is Products Sourcing?

Product Sourcing is the way of finding sources of products to sell. If you you're going to own a Home-base Internet Business, you need to have a source of products, you need to be sure you can buy those products at a true wholesaler price so that you can make profit when you sell them to your customers at your retail price. But most real wholesale supplier will not work with you, because as a small business we do not have the money to order thousands of pounds worth of products at one time. A wholesale supplier's business is base on volume sales that means they have to sell a lot of products in order to make money. They simply won't sell to anyone who can't afford to purchase a minimum order ranging from £5,000 to £20,000 or more. They do not consider it to worth their effort. That's why most of Internet lists of wholesalers are useless, and those printed companies listed are not even in the business anymore. They are jam-packet with middlemen ready to charge too much for the products you want. When a wholesaler gets to well know on the internet, they become overexpose to millions of people, and that creates too much competition for their products for anyone to make a good profit. So the wholesales that do this are trying to expand their sales by making it as easy as possible to sell their products online, because they are not ecommerce the end up making things harder for customers. If they do have ecommerce, the problem is that they have to use a couple of employees to run the business and pay for that somehow. As we know, you can't sell products if you do not have any, and your product sourcing is the Lifeblood of your Online Business.

Where to Find a Wholesaler?

When you're starting Internet business you're looking for wholesalers who are:

o   True Wholesale Suppliers
o   Not Overexposed on Internet
o   Do not sell extras internet package
o   Do not make things harder for their customer.

So you have to go to the Sources, not to the middlemen, and using multiple sourcing methods that will make you more successful, than using only one. It is very important to do it right for your business. This is the kind of research that at Connecting Enterprise Ltd, we have been doing for many year to find most trusted products sourcing tool. When you deal with Product Sourcing, you are looking for True Drop Shippers, Large Volume Suppliers, Liquidators, Light Bulk Wholesalers and Importers who will work with small home base Internet business.

If you want to make drop shipping work for you, start developing the websites before you approach the drop-shipping manufacturer. Focus all your efforts on some niche and create a website or a network of websites around your niche, to dominate the market. With e-source you can set up many ecommerce stores or you can use sites like elance.com to recruit all kinds of talents.

Having said this, we feel that success requires uniqueness and extra effort from your part that will set you aside from falling. I believe that hard work, dedication and passion are the key elements to success.

And if you approach manufacturers or any supplier like almost everyone else does as: *will you drop ship for me?*' or *what is your price list?* Then you will receive an equally short reply and even no reply at all from them. If you want to be considered seriously, present yourself to the drop shipper seriously with a professional business proposal, with a ready website, and you will have their full attention.

IMPORTING FROM CHINA

If you are interested in importing goods from China, you'll need to know about some of the special considerations that trading with China can present for your company. We will focus on the special nature of working with China. China is an enormous country and it is not realistic to assume that any guideline will address all business practices. However, before you run in and place an order, there are certain guidelines you should follow and precautions you should take into account. You can learn more at create-to-succeed. co.uk. Let's begin with the matter of the cultural differences in how business is conducted in China. But if you are a newbie, it's better to purchase products from your country instead of jumping to importing from overseas; the risk is to higher from unknown country.

Relation And Business Culture

Since China has opened its doors to trade relatively recently, many business people do not yet have experience in working with the Eastern approach to business relationships. The Chinese business world operates somewhat differently from businesses in many Western and African cultures. This lack of shared knowledge may feel intimidating, but like many countries, China, places enormous value on relationships as the blood of business building. Chinese business people prefer to begin business dealings by getting to know their business partners. If you run a small business and cannot afford to travel to China for face-to-face meetings it is a difficult prospect for you. However, there are some ways that you can foster a relationship with your Chinese counterpart, even at a distance. Keep in mind that the Chinese language has no tenses and the phrase must be interpreted from context. So, when Chinese people speak just a little English, they can mix up tenses or use none when they actually mean past or future. Speak slowly and avoid using jargon so that your Chinese counterparts have a better opportunity to understand you.

If you do have the opportunity to meet your suppliers in person, smile and shake hands but recognise that the Chinese handshake is much less firm than the Western handshake.

Expect to be entertained and to host some entertainment. Recognise that white is the colour of mourning in China; it's not an appropriate overall colour to wear even in the hot, southern portions of the country. Be prepared for people to smoke in all environments and expect less eye contact.

China is a country that bases a good deal of its behaviour on issues of respect. You can show your respect for this way of thinking by:

Acting more formally, less casually in correspondence, conversation and use of names, or understand and follow the company hierarchy. Remember that the Chinese will use your hierarchy. They will expect to be introduced to the most senior person first and will feel more secure if they have communicated with the most senior person in your organisation. If you intend to use a representative in your dealings with your Chinese supplier, a subordinate employee or an import agent, introduce that person to the supplier's management in order to confer your trust in that person's representation. The more respect are given to the older person.

Business Negotiation

Whenever you are approaching a new country for a business, adapted yourself to the culture of the country to facilitate your negotiation. One of the most common mistakes that Westerners make in working with the Chinese is in the way they approach business negotiations.

Here is the way to act.

When you hear the word yes, it does not necessarily mean, 'I agree' it may mean, 'Yes, I know what you are saying or I understand what you are talking about'. Confirm in writing any understanding that you believe you have reached. Some Chinese businessmen do not view a contract as a final, binding agreement. The contract is often just a milestone in negotiations that will be revisited and changed. Of course, the contract may in fact be a legal binding agreement but you must understand that you will need to pursue legal recourse to enforce the terms, a situation that may not be worth the time and money. Anticipate this situation by developing a strong personal relationship and being sure that your contract serves both parties well enough to reduce the need for changes.

Chinese business people are not afraid of silences and use their willingness to remain silent during a negotiation to encourage you to essentially negotiate against yourself. Don't fall into this trap. Either returns the silence or restates your position and requests a response.

Expect that establishing agreements will take longer as your Chinese counterparts consider your proposals. On the other hand, the Chinese will think you are wasting time or don't trust if you spend too much time with legal tinkering.

Remember that China is probably in a time zone that is very different from your, it uses only one time zone even though the country is enormous. Make yourself a chart of times and figure out when you can make contact with your Chinese partners during working time.

Avoid trying to get much done other than already established operations during February, the time of the Chinese New Year. This is a major time of celebration in China, similar to the Christmas holidays in other countries. Little business is transacted, either in private industry or through the government.

Shipping Terms

*Incoterm*s is an abbreviation of International Commercial Terms, an international system of abbreviations that serve to communicate the division of responsibilities for transport, delivery, costs and insurance between the buyer and the seller. To verified go to www.iccwbo.org for an in-depth discussion of terms and meanings.

Remember, the incoterms are not meant to replace statements in a contract of sale that outline transfers of ownership or title to goods. As a result, the incoterms may not be useful to resolve disputes regarding payment or ownership of goods.

As you might expect, while Chinese business people share some common characteristics, there are significant differences in approach to business relationships across regions.

Product Selection

Chinese products are very inexpensive in large part because there is such an enormous, minimally paid labour pool. The average total labour compensation for a Chinese manufacturing worker is 0.57 pound per hour, with many making far less than that benefits included.

Importing goods process involves pre-registering for vat. It is important to understand vat because you may have to comply with vat regulations, paying and collecting vat and reconciling vat transactions with the government. This section gives an in-depth explanation of VAT and Excise tax.

Registration for VAT

To register for vat when your business is located in UK, you will need to fill out a vat registration form www.hmrc.gov.uk. You should receive a certificate of registration showing your full registration details within four weeks. You must start keeping records and charging VAT to your customers from the date you know you have to be registered.

If you import goods regularly, you can establish an account with HMRC that allows you to pay one lump sum by direct debit each month. This means that payments don't have to be handled for each transaction, so goods are often cleared more efficiently. Setting up an account is free, but requires a bank guarantee

Compliance With Company VAT

When your company becomes VAT registered you must comply with the VAT regulations that affect your business. The key requirements are: VAT records including invoices and receipts should be kept for a 6 years period.

Receipts for VAT-included business purchases are the evidence you will need to claim a VAT refund. Notify HM Revenue and Customs within 30 days of any relevant changes in your business information. Charge VAT on supplies made to the company's employees or inter-company transactions. Provide your customer with a vat invoice, when you sell goods or services that incorporate a vat charge. Your customers need vat invoices to reclaim, as input tax, the vat you have charged them.

Explanation of VAT

If you are importing goods into your country you will pay VAT on those goods. You will then need to charge VAT for those goods and report your payments and collections to the government agency in charge of VAT collections. VAT is a tax on consumption; it is collected on imports, acquisitions and business transactions. The objective of vat is to place a tax on the end consumer of a product or service. You should remain VAT-neutral, unless you are the end user of the imported commodities. For example when goods are imported into the UK from outside the EU, VAT is normally due at the same rate as on a supply of those goods in the UK. VAT is charged as a percentage of prices, around 20%.

Chapter 10

PRACTICAL EXERCISES

Part1
<u>**Case1**</u>**: Selling Sex Toys**

Your cost of Sex Toys item from your supplier is:

£2.00 including delivery. Let us assume that the product you are importing has a UK duty on import for this example of 10% you will need to determine the duty applicable to your product by consulting the Tariff Classification Service (TCS). The UK VAT is around 20% for most goods.

*£2 cost of item + 10% import duty £2 = £2 + £0.2 = 2.2 therefore import duty = £2.2-£2 cost item£0.2 VAT import £2.2+20%VAT x (cost +import) £2.2= £2.2+ £0.44 = 2.64 therefore VAT= £2.64-£2.2 = £0.44 Therefore £2.64 is the cost to you after product cost from manufacturer + delivery + duties + VAT._You take the decision to sell the product at £10+ VAT at 20% of £10) =£10 + 20% * £10 = £12 your selling price*

You will need to pay to the government agency in charge of VAT collections, the VAT you charged on your sale price minus the VAT you already paid when you imported the goods:

£12 (selling price)—£10 (selling price ex VAT)= £2 total VAT at time of selling £2-£0.44 (VAT already paid on import) = £1.56 VAT still due to the government.

Your profit is then: the sale price (£12), minus the duty (£0.20), minus the VAT on import (£0.44), minus the VAT returned after selling the item (£1.56), minus the actual cost of the item (£2.00): £12.00-£0.20-£0.44-£1.56-£2.00 = £7.8 profit.

With Drop shipping, your customers can change their mind within 15 days after delivery. In the fashion e-commerce, return rates are particularly high, and can reach up to 30%. At that level, returns can have very negative effects on the net margin and the good will of your Company:

The wrong size and wrong colours as expected in the first place.

As a key of your success, you must offer your customers great shopping experience, painless and comfortable.

To optimize your marketing cost, every acquired customer, must be turned into a «renewing-customer».

To succeed in this, you must offer a solid after sales service, including a very flexible return policy.

Case2: Selling Jeans *considers you sell 20 jeans in 1 month.*

*Your selling price: £50, with a buying price: £25. So an immediate gross profit of £25 * 20 pcs = £500.*

5 customers requested to exchange size, and 2 others want to return & refund.

=> *Let's solve the 5 jeans to change size:*

- *You collect the items from your customer (5 * £25 = £125, value in Stock)*
- *You order 5 new jeans to exchange sizes. (5 * £25 = £125, Debit from bank account)*
- *And you also need to deal with the 5 jeans that have been returned to you, to turn them into Cash flow.*

=> *Now let's solve the 2 jeans that customers request return & refund:*

- *You collect the items back (2 * £25 = £50, value in Stock)*
- *You refund the customers the price of their initial invoice: 2 * 50 = £100, Debit from bank account.*

Return policy cost: Money blocked in Stock; £175 + Total Debit from bank account; £225

Balance: Gross profit of £500—Total Debit from bank account; £225 = Cash flow in bank; £275 + £175 in blocked stock.

VAT Registration Requirements

You must register to participate in the VAT system if: At the end of any month the total value of the taxable supplies you have made (sold) in the past twelve months or less is more than the current threshold (£70,000); and at any time you expect that the value of your taxable supplies will be more than the current registration threshold (£70,000) in the next thirty days alone.

You can also register for VAT on a voluntary basis, even if you do not currently qualify under the thresholds. Some businesses do this in order to reclaim VAT on purchases they make, effectively saving 20%. Of course, you will also have to pass along the VAT to your purchasers, raising the price by 20%. If the majority of your customers are businesses, they will simply make the same claim. If, however, you are selling to individuals, they must pay the tax so the price of your product effectively remains at a 20% increase. You should analyse your own situation and determine whether or not voluntary registration makes sense for your company.

Part2
A Million Pound Business plan turnover:

*Let me show you how all these systems work to create a very simple plan that work for every entrepreneur or business owner who wants to build **Total-Money-Tree-Machine-Business** a system that never stop to bring you money.*

In internet time and social media, there are a lot of new opportunities, and there will be more new millionaires every year. So, look around you and see what you can create:

Book/e-Books—Audio Programs—Online Courses—Skype Coaching—Seminar—Webinars—Drop Shipping Business—Fulfilment By Amazon Business.

In traditional way of doing business, you need big money to start a business like: Import Export, Refurbishing IT, Refurbishing Cloths and a lot more. My own business is base on drop shipping, fulfilment by Amazon and Online Training Programme.

A—Traditional Business Model to adapt in Internet time

This plan was created for Jonathan a businessman; one of my best friend who asked me one day, Jean I need a plan for my new business base in Malawi to make a million pounds in 12 months and I want to be able to do it without building a huge infrastructure or hopping to look for tens of thousands of new clients.

In almost every industry, this would be quite a big challenging problem for a manager to achieve and me to write a business plan. In internet time and new way of doing business, it is fairly straightforward. Anyway I show this client that he can accomplish his dream with just 40 Independents Representatives and four hundred customers, without staff, and just the following four basic work efforts.

1a—Refurbishing Products.

Let say Jonathan choose to sale second hand Products: Cloths, Bags and Shoes.

1—Create a list of products that you want to sale and product sourcing.

Now you have your product sourcing, create a small video recording the product and some comment how they worked and how their products are usefully and good and all the condition they're using to satisfy their customers all over the world.

2—Ccreate a group of 40 Independents Representatives who will find customer that will buy from you.

Give every representative a DVD that you have recorded to present to your future customer in a small meeting every month.

3—Create a choice price product

First I told Jonathan to create a priced items product. Of course he was wondering what does this mean. I'm sure you have the envy to know, so I will be defining my term as we move through this plan.

*In the industry of second hand products (Cloths and Shoes etc) products are list on category: Class **A** high price, Class **B** Medium-price and Class **C** or **D** Lower-price.*

*Let's assume that Jonathan has created all this process and want to move directly and efficiently step by step from point **A** to point **B**. Now we have to know how much he wants to invest in this business.*

***Remember**: During the month that Jonathan is selling his categoty1 container, he's already order a category2 container for the next month and the category3 for the third one. The cycle of shipping will be every month knowing that to ship a container from Europe to Africa is taking about 21 days to 28 days.*

Jonathan has £36,000 to invest in his new business of selling second hand cloths, bag and shoes in Malawi.

He just buys a 40 inch container of second hand bags and belts first choice (Class A) with 400 ballots of 55kgs each. The cost of product, transport (FOB) and customer duty is £32,650.

Now let get the numbers if Jonathan sells just one container a month through his 40 representatives at a price set on different three categories of products that we are going to talk about.

Category1—Container 40 Inch of Second Hand Bags and Belts with 400 ballots

A)—First month shipping Category1 container of 40 Inch

This is £193 x 400 = £77,200 a month.

If Jonathan ship 4 containers of Category1 per year, everyone of his 40 representatives only need to have a list of 10 customers each month, this mean that the representative need to find 2 customers every 4 days to build his list for only 20 days a month and these are 400 customers brought by his representatives.

This category1 will make him £77,200 x 4 = £308,800 a year not bad and he only need 40 people to do it 4 times a year.

Category 2—Container 40 Inch of Second Hand Cloths with 400 ballots

B)—Second month shipping Category2 container of 40 Inch

This is £ 187 x 400 = £ 74,800 a month.

Let say Jonathan ships 4 containers of Category2 per year, using the same process we build in first shipping, this category2 will bring him.

£74,800 x 4 = £ 299,200 a year not bad and he only uses 40 people to do the job for him 4 times a year.

Category 3—Container 40 Inch of Second Hand Shoes with 400 ballots

C)—Third month shipping Category3 container of 40 Inch

This is £ 197 x 400 = £ 78,800 a month.

Let Jonathan ships 4 containers of Category3 per year, using the same process, this category will bring him: £78,800 x 4 = £ 315200 a year not bad at all, he uses only 40 people to do the job for him.

At this point, let me address the ignorance of sceptics. Many newbies or outsider would say, hey guy, who would ever pay £ 187 for a ballot of second hand product like this when you can get cloths shoes etc from Chinese shops in the same area? What these types of question display is a general lack of understanding about the business and the real need of customers. Customer on this side of planet still love to wear western products and trust them more than what Chinese are selling. The quality of items found in second hand cloths are some time invaluable in term of price.

2a—Create a Low-priced of subscription program.

So now we have Jonathan up to:

£ 308,800 a year on category1 + £ 299,200 a year on category2 + £ 315200 a year on category3, doing it when he does not looking for any customer. The job is done by others people; we call it delegating the work to someone else.

On top of this I suggested he create a subscription member through the representatives, we called it a continuity monthly program, where he sends information to representative one a month about the new products and the shipping day. So any representative can supply the message to their list of clients. I also suggested to host 2 days every month a small workshop with his customers how to sale and where to boost them, when he still waiting the delivery of container.

This is a low-tier priced in this business, now Jonathan can charge £ 17.97 to £ 30 every month to his customers to attend his training. I suggested starting at £21.00 a subscription.

Look at the number, if Jonathan gets all his 400 customers through his representatives to pay £21 per month for his training, he will be earning and extra of £ 21x 400 = £ 8400 a month which equal an astounding £ 8,400 x 12 = £ 100,800 per year.

Imagine making £ 100,800 a year with just 400 clients brought by others people when you don't have to work very hard. Now keep in mind that you don't have to do workshop every month but it important because it brought you and extra money which is enough to pay all of your representatives if each received £200 per monthly transaction. You can do a video but you do not need to personally create the content yourself. You could hire a freelancer to do the job or create a training video to you. Nowadays you could even speak to a small group on the list of any of your representatives doing skype coaching, to motivate your customer that is it.

With all these strategies in place, we have created an entire new millionaire business empire from scratch for Jonathan by doing just four things. This is Total-Money-Tree-Machine-Business that never stop. Let's look at how all these numbers add up.

1. *If Jonathan sells just his Category1 Container 40 Inch of Second Hand Bags and Belts with 400 ballots at £193 each, he would earn £ 77200 a month and £ 308,800 a year.*

2. *If Jonathan just sells his Category2 Container 40 Inch of Second Hand Cloths with 400 ballots at £187 each, he would earn £ 74,800 a month and £ 299,200 a year.*

3. *If Jonathan just sells his Category3 Container 40 Inch of Second Hand Shoes with 400 ballots at £197 each, he would earn £ 78,800 a month and £ 315200 a year.*

4. *If Jonathan just sells only a low-tier membership training to all his representatives list of clients he will be earning and extra of £ 8400 a month which equal an astounding £ 100,800 a year*

Combined these four strategies earn Jonathan £ 1,032,000 a year!!

Jonathan was in his way of making a horrible decision in hiring many people like others, he was following the advice of traditional business men/women and investors who have no idea of how this model of business work.

What's remarkable about this plan is that, it doesn't require Jonathan to have tens upon of tens of products or thousands upon thousands of clients. He needs only four sales strategies and tactics, 40 Independents Representatives with 10 customers each, for people to by from him. To become a millionaire, he needs to sell one container at wholesale prise a month for 12 months and 2 days workshops training a month.

My goal in illustrating this simple plan is to show an example of how with just a few product and a little strategies, tactics, can add up to a big opportunity.

Of course you've finished with Jonathan business model which is a traditional way of doing business that need a big Money and I hope you enjoy it.

Now in Internet business, you do not need a big money to start your business. You can enter the entrepreneurial expert industry of internet time and social media. Becoming an expert is simply a matter of positioning, packaging, promoting and who you are and what you know so that you can help other people in your target niche. In this model I will show you how to do it.

What I'm talking about is not that you becoming an expert in order to become a *knowledge worker* for some corporation creating global company. The knowledge worker is a long-dead concept and in Internet time fuelled by content, authenticity, search engines, and social media, the new class of entrepreneurs and experts will work for themselves and create real relationships with people based on valuable advice and information. Why? Because of the great liberalisation of content and distribution that internet has brought to the world, every one of us can create and distribute a valuable information and content that help other people to live a better life. You are about to discover that in this Total-Money-Tree-Machine-Business. I will show you a Million-pound internet plan for getting your business out there and getting paid for it that may surprise you in the simplicity of its implementation.

Having said all this, I know that my words might sound unbelievable to you. So my aim in this book is to teach you about this entrepreneurial expert industry, and make these three arguments to you in such a *concrete, rational and implemental* way so that, *you can stop dreaming and start living the dream, inspiring others how to succeed in life.*

Mark Zuckerberg has turned his simple idea of facebook to a business empire and built more than ten billions pounds with billion of people around the world.

Tony Robbins has been inspiring people to find their personal power for thirty years, and he has reached millions of people around the world and built a £40,000,000 empire under his brand in the process.

You see, One Direction, these young guys came to X-Factor the Reality TV Show to express their talent. None of them knew each until they were putting together by judges to form a Boy Band. Now they are famous, they did not even win the show. They wanted to be there and work hard in that industry, so they mastered their learning to deliver music that customer would buy.

John Gray took a simple idea that men and women often seem like they're on different planets and turn it into a three-decade phenomenon of books, coaching, speeches, workshops and online videos that men are from Mars, women are from Venus Empire.

In fact, many of these people are now *household* names, and recognise all over the world. What is important to know about these examples is that none of these people started rich and famous. They start just like you and me. What they did next was build their expertise, learn how to positioning, packaging promote and partner with other, and figure out a way to serve as many people as they could.

People will always need help and advice in their personal and professional lives. Every generation needs career advice, business advice, spiritual advice, technology advice, financial advice, love advice and so on. There is no limit to how many people search for and need your knowledge and information. As an entrepreneurial expert, you can find your way of serving people with care, compassion and consistency on one of the topic below. You can work anywhere at anytime; remember when Tim Ferris wrote the 4-Hour Workweek, he had know idea how big it would get or how many people would find his way of seeing things completely unbelievable. The same thing happened to Robert Kiyosaki when he wrote Poor Dad Rich Dad.

B—Million-Pounds Business Plan As Entrepreneurial Expert

Now let me show you how you can put together all these topics to create a very simple plan, to build a million-pounds business as entrepreneurial expert. This second plan was create for a small private group of fifteen people brought by Jonathan and each paid me £1,947. At the time this project was created, I was talking about Entrepreneurial Expert Industry, the new way of doing business. In fact I showed Jonathan and his group that they could accomplish their goal with just hundreds of customers, without staff and with just the following five basic efforts.

1—Create a low-price information product

In this industry a low-price product is anything in the £25-£199 range, and information product is basically training material with your advice or strategies and tactics for success packaged into an educational product. This information product is often a book, e-Book, CD audio programme online training or DVD home-study course in any topic that you have mastered.

Let say that Jonathan creates an audio program comprised of just five CD that sells for £197. An audio programme like this is easy to create in Internet time. Jonathan needs to buy a good microphone and plug into his computer with free or paid software on his computer, and just record his voice on the subject he masters as training. All he needs to do is to spend five hours recording one-hour session, which automatically becoming five CDs in his audio training. Once he has the MP4 files from his recordings, he can send them to a CD manufacturer and have them create his CDs and product design. Yes, Jonathan has a product now, which the manufacturer prints on demand and fulfils. Now all Jonathan needs is a website to sell the training programme.

Now, let's look the numbers. If Jonathan sells just one pack of programme a day at £198 in standard 30 day a month, he would earn £5,940 a month, multiply that amount by 12 months, and this product can make him £71,280 a year and only needed 360 customers to achieve it.

At this point don't let yourself smothered by the ignorance of some and barren criticisms. Many newbies or outside observers would try to discourage you by saying that "Oh Jean who would ever pay £198 for an audio training programme when you can get tape or book/e-Book for £15?" This kind of question is lack of knowledge about entrepreneurial expert industry. In this industry is not how much it costs to create the product, but how much value it delivers. Expertise is not a commodity like toothpaste is. For instant a five CDs audio programme can be manufactured and done for around £10-£20, but it's certainly worth more than that if it solves someone's problems or improve people life or business. Yes, as an example I bought a CD **Plan For Life of Financial Success of Rich Dad Education at £29,99 and** *a* **DVD of Les Brown motivational speaker** *around £169 a few years ago and it help me change the way I do think. Is a life change worth £29.99 + £169? So I think that anyone who does not is simply not your customer.*

Let's move on and see how the pound starts adding up in this business model.

2—Create a low-price membership program

Now we have Jonathan up to £71,280 a year by selling a £198 audio training programme. On top of this I suggested he create a membership subscription where he host monthly training and answered questions as well. In this step, Jonathan can charge £21 all the way to £63 base on her position and know-how. To access the video, his clients could login to a member site only and download the video and audio recordings.

Looking at the numbers, if Jonathan gets only 100 people a month to pay £63 a month for this, he would be earning

£6,300 extra money per month, which equals £75,600 per year. Imagine a £75,600 a year with just 100 customers a month, and all you need to do is send out a video and host a call once a month. In entrepreneurial expert industry it happens when all the time, you're delivering excellent value and content to your customers. Now do you see how fast this all adds up?

Let's keep tracking our way to £1,000,000.

3—Create a medium-price product

Next, I asked Jonathan to consider making an advance comprehensive training that show Hairdresser the hidden business that lay in their business and how to implement it without investing more than £1,000.

Let's say Jonathan created a £597 DVD home-study course on his topic about hidden business that lay in hairdressers business that could have them earn more money with less effort and the danger of constantly being standing up, use of chemical product and of scissor that affect their health.

This home-study course for Hairdresser to earn more money with a hidden business could include 8 DVDs, transcripts, a workbook and a bonus of 2 UBS audio programme. If he sold 50 units a month just less than two a day, that would equal £29, 850 a month, which add s up to bringing £358,200 a year. Remember, I'm not asking Jonathan to sell thousands of units but only 50 clients a month in this case; he then pockets £358,200 a year with just this one product. The average British wage is less than £33,500 so this is incredible by most of people's standards.

Notice that we are just getting warmed up. Because all those people whose lives have been transformed by Jonathan's audio, subscription and DVD programmes will want to see his live event one day, they will want to go to his workshop or seminar.

4—Create a High multi workshop and seminar

Running seminar is a lucrative business for entrepreneurial expert. Look around you and think about any guru you've ever followed, they have a seminar or live workshop event. Let's imagine that Jonathan plans to launch two seminars a year, one with hairdressers exclusively and another with all his clients. He plans all year and gets 100 hairdressers for the first workshop and another100 customers for his second seminar.

A) *Let say that Jonathan charges each one £1000 to attend 6 days workshops on hidden business that lay in hairdressers business. They paid that amount because it is Jonathan live in person with full of best content how to move directly and efficiently step by step from point A to point B to achieve a specific outcome. And Jonathan have 12 months to persuade 100 hairdressers to come to his workshop, this would earn him £100,000 in ticket sales. We are not counting the Back End sales, which would be additional product and programme that customer's purchase at the live event.*

B) *In the second seminar Jonathan manages to get 150 customers into his seminar of 4 days, each one paying £797 to participate. They do it of course it is Jonathan programme that help people to change their life for a better or to make their business work hard for them and work less. Jonathan would earn another £119550 year for just*

4 days. Remember we are not mentioning the back end of a seminar, which often worth more than the front end.

5—Create a medium—price product on Drop shipping or fulfilment by Amazon business.

The Drop shipping business is another way of doing business without having to buy any stock, handling, packing and shipping. The only things Jonathan needs to do it is to look for a legitimate drop shipper wholesaler or supplier, promote their product in his website or another plate form, and sells them as retailer price an make profit.

Let's say Jonathan build a website to sell a set of suite and shoes to a specific niche of his customers at special price. Every month he manages to get 70 customers each one paying £350 for the set of suites and shoes bought on his website, Jonathan would pocket £24,500 a month and this is £294,000 a year for his specific niche of customer without having to buy any stock of product. We are not adding others product he could be selling.

With this last strategy in place, we have created an entire new millionaire business empire from scratch for Jonathan and his group by doing just five things. This is another Total-Money-Tree-Machine Business that never stops. Let's look at how all these numbers come together.

1- If Jonathan sells just one low-price audio programme a day at £198, he would earn£5,940 a month and **£71,280** a year.
2- If Jonathan gets only 100 people a month to pay £63 a month for membership programme, he would be

earning £6,300 extra money per month, which equals **£75,600** per year.

3- If Jonathan sells just 50 units medium-price product a month at £597 DVD home study for Hairdresser to earn more money with a hidden business, that would equal £29, 850 a month, which adds up to bringing him **£358,200** a year.

4- If Jonathan sells just 100 workshops tickets to hairdressers at £1000, he would pocket £100,000 a year. If Jonathan manages to get 150 clients to his second seminar at £797, he would earn another £119,550 a year.

5- If Jonathan sells only 70 set of suite and shoes at £350 each, he pockets a month, with no stock he would earn **£294,000** a year.

Joined, these five strategies and tactics together earn Jonathan £1,018,640 a year

Of course, this is just a sample plan, and there are plenty of ways to reach a million pounds business. Jonathan could decide to do Drop Shipping Business, Fulfilment By Amazon (FBA) Business or something else.

At this point, I know many people have negative opinions to all of this. They say "Well Jean not everyone can do business like this." To this I reply, "Why not"? In internet time anyone can be whatever he wants if he really wants to achieve a financial freedom by learning and mastering a topic, right. You can organise your knowledge into helpful advice. And these days, anyone can put up a website and offer their know-how for sale. So what is all the mystery about making money? I hope this book help debunking this myth and blockage.

Chapter 11

MY WORKING DAY BEFORE DISCOVERING DROP-SHIPPING & FBA

Everyone is Busy Plan your day job!

My work schedule was a little relaxed when I started, I had not left my job as a production operator in the factory. My written and video training are designed to help people who wish to open their own business online, without having websites or blogs, but also create a real lucrative business on Internet without knowing anything about it. It is as clear as the spring water and feasible from anyone who wants to be financial free. It is with great pleasure that I would like to provide you with examples of practices, some of my failures but more importantly how you go about achieving the success you deserve in your business on Internet without a turbo marketing or social networks knowledge.

You will see that, there is really nothing special, you just simply follow the process and apply the practical methodology. "If you do not take action, you can never know if you are going to Succeed or Fail!"

The best way to find out is not to invest 80% or 100% of your time in this new business, but just give 20% of your time and energy, the 80% are already being provided by training course and just apply what you see. It is only in this way that you will be able to take your destiny and change your life forever!

Here's my schedule for a day's work when I was still a factory worker where I worked four days a week and four days off. About 3 days a week I was focus on my own business, you will find that I always have a bit of free time.

During my normal working day

As I said in P15 when I started, my day starts with a loud sound of an alarm clock, I was waking up at 5:30 am, going to my regular job, coming home at 7:30 pm and then I would work on my online business from 09:00 pm to 01:00 am. Then wake up at 5:30 am for work again the next day.

I was busting my ass everyday trying to get this online thing to work and I was working two jobs, my regular job plus my online business. I was doing everything myself, from the design, to the marketing, to the copywriting and videos coupled with the fact that I did not know how, I would teach myself through hours of google researches with lot of frustration when things were going wrong.

During my four days off

8:30: I get up and took my shower, get ready, drank my chocolate gently took the time to breathe and get to my office which was in my home whereabout I was running my business www.connecting-enterprise.co.uk. This is where I wrote most of my training, created video and wrote business strategies.

9:30: I start my day job where I read e-mails that I received one day ago until morning so that my clients or potential buyers of one of my products get a very quick response on my part.

10:00: I watch orders that arrived day before in the afternoon and until early morning and prepare packages for shipment. I brought a particular attention to the preparation of my products, their packaging and labelling with the exact address of the recipient. This entire job was done when I was selling physical product pack in my home, before I start Drop Shipping and Fulfilment by Amazon.

11:00: Once my packages are ready I realise at the post office which is located very close to my home, chat with postman/woman and leave my package to be shipping.

12:00: I come back to my desk; I make the sale of unsold items whose sales were completed in the previous day. If I have received new products in the afternoon, I take a picture; write sale text that describes the product accurately.

13:30: It was the moment that I prefer, because I was looking for new products that have a potential niche. I'm looking for the best suppliers of the product I want to add on my sites, I can contact new suppliers to see details with them and decide whether or not to order.

14:30: I make tests on my texts sales; I take new pictures that put further highlight the products I market. I add other ads on classifieds sites ads with different pictures and text. For instance, if you sell physical products. Take picture with a digital camera or a phone and transfer them to your computer. Current mobile phones perform great pictures. Do not buy a digital camera if you have a phone like Smartphone, iPhone, iPad . . .

15H30/16h30: My job stops there. Mostly I have the whole afternoon to practice my favourite hobby, go shopping, and do some paperwork administrative sometimes. Most of the time, except the period of rush time I finished my day of work and I am free for the rest of the day.

At the end of the day I like to go and check my E-mail to answer to my clients, or prospective buyers to quickly check that all goes well. It takes me between 30 and 45 minutes, and I have peace of mind for the evening.

That looks like a schedule with different variants few times, because in the business world it is not "all white" or "all black" and you should know to adapt to different circumstances that may happened.

This is one of my typical days, you are free to organize the way you want, especially if it is a first time, you do not need to spend all your time as a professional seller on Internet.

Once your business is up and depending on the extent you want to give, you will spend more time. Personally, the goal I have set myself was to organise my working time as I want to enjoy my free time to carry onto my other occupations and future projects.

I did all this work without leaving my work at CooperVision as production operator, this job was a sort of starting block for me to move efficiently. It is very Energetic and this is happiness, I was always more motivated. Starts now don't waste time it's "a win-win business."

How a Turbo Seller chooses its products to sell in a few clicks?

What to sell? What is your speciality?

You will sell more on Internet, through marketplaces, if you become a supplier of specific types of products and good quality; so your customers (who need your products) will come back and will remain faithful to you until they find cheaper elsewhere. However, if you selle products of very poor quality, your potential buyers will runaway and those you have purchased this product before will give bad assessments. When you think that you need to sell, there is some essential points to consider. The most important of them is to always offer a product that you know the quality and performances. It's like watching a great football match.

You will come easier to talk about if you pleased it or if you did not like at all. In sales, it's the same thing. If you do not know well or very little the product you are trying to sell, you will make a very poor description and you will market the product not at the best price. So, conversely, if you're talking about the same product with great conviction and so very positive, you will increase your sales, and more you will market your product at a better price. This is how you increase your profits, choose the right products, know their benefits and their qualities and highlight with beautiful ads and beautiful pictures (as well as the ad title percussion).

How to select a product to sell?

Look what products sell best (Google search to find statistic) and look the best supplier for this product.

Select of course a product that give you a comfortable margin on each sale. Opt for products that are easy to ship by post. A consumable product is even better because people will ordered it again when it is consumed. Do not sell the electronic products because you fancy it, competition is very rude to make any good profit. Be aware that collection products have high demand!

The products that are not important to sell Mostly?

Products that come out of the Euro zone for Europeans. Avoid wherever possible to sell branded products, unless you use Fulfilment By Amazon. Moreover, I explain this method in my training web site www.create-to-succeed.co.uk how to do it. The products have to be Shipped Directly by the Representative of the Brand to Amazon Fulfilment Centre. Leave aside the sale of perfume, or strong alcohol prohibited on many platforms due to counterfeiting.

Do not sell digital books, also for most of them, the license included within forbid you to promote the platforms. In addition, there are few platforms that will empower you to offer such products. Examples of platforms that prohibit sales of such products are: eBay, Amazon, Priceminister, Leboncoin. Besides you will not earn much with digital products sold a few pound out there. When you start, do not sell bulky products which can not be shipped directly from your own effort. Do not sell either counterfeit because you may have very big problems with customers, customs services and kill your own business.

As I said in the beginning of this book, information has monetary value and the secret of Internet business is to have good and true information and then the necessary tools you need. Have you ever heard about the three German brothers who have a wildly successful business model? In a nutshell, they find a successful internet business in the US, and then clone it. Their cloning all starts with one of their business base in Berlin called Rocket Internet, in total, the brother have launched more than 100 companies. Their **Zalando, a clone of "Zappos"** now dominates six European markets. You too can have your online business.

In the full version of the training how to create your Internet Business Empire, I reveal how to highlight your products and disseminate your ads so that your products sell more quickly and at a better price, without losing any penny from your pocket to put your ads. You can exceed all your competitors.

If you want to drive a car you need to learn the theory and past the test; so you can go to practical training. Here the difference between Learning to Drive and this Business Model is that:

You do not need to learn any Theory.
You go Straight to Practical process, which is copy and paste step-by-step.
Duplicate or clone what you see.
No Stress, No Headache, No Time wasting.
This is a shortcut to get things done with immediate outcome

Don't forget, the value of this learning is so great than amount of your investment. Imagine being able to clone a successful business for yourself? I can't promise that you're going to succeed at 100%, because if you are not active nothing will happen.

But the truth and good thing I guarantee you is that: the system work 100% because other people are using it to succeed, they just follow how to implement the business. That is what we are doing in my own business. Don't follow those who will try to bring you down; we are living in the world of hypocrisy. The evangelist Matthew will say: "Man's enemies will be those of his household".

Anyway, it's certainly true that not everyone will become a millionaire or achieving a financial freedom. My aim here is to help people to change their mind of seeing things, but not to guarantee everyone will. I'm often asked, "Jean, your example for making money is great, but can anyone do the same and become financially free?" as a messenger of strategies, I will say that my achievements are not typical and that no one is guaranteed to earn an income by following my training or strategies. But what I've noticed as Dan Kennedy say is that,

"Every successful enterprise, whether it's on Internet Business or Traditional Venture has an unmistakable secret formula. Why? Because the natural laws that govern our universe are not done for some people, anyone who applies exactly the secret formula of success for a given enterprise can expect the same success that others have achieved by applying the same secret formula."

The truth is that we all have different levels of skill, ambition, talent, knowledge, ability, attitude, resources and commitment to succeed, so, anyway we are all going to get different achievements in life and some are happy where they are and you can change their mind. I personally do not think anyone in life is guaranteed anything; we do have to just take a risk, and it's unfair to guarantee your learner any results with your teaching. That makes sense to me.

This book comes to the end, now you can stop dreaming and start living the dream. I wish you to apply The Jean Secret Formula to Get Ahead $[F^2 = (V + A + R) \times O + (D + HW)]$ and start "right" with joy and happiness. I hope to have the pleasure to help you go further with training "Create your own Internet business empire without the need of a bank loan or a Premiership footballer salary".

Therefore you must choose how you want to spend your time and energy, either on activities that generate an abundance of money, work for big corporations companies or on activities that make a significant contribution to others and get paid for.

AN OFFER FROM JEAN TCHAMGUE

For reader of this Book

Dear reader,

Thank you so much for having this book. I hope that you read this book as soon as you get it. You see I had never imagined being a Publisher author; in fact I had to be encouraged and pushed into putting the pen to paper and sharing my story. I remember sitting in my tiny cold room in Portsmouth, asking myself: How can I make a real impact when I have to work hard just to make an income in life? How can I get my message out there and really influence others in deep and meaningful way? Now you've finished this book, together we will breakthrough the money barrier. This can be the beginning or the end of story.

If you've enjoyed my book and found it useful, then I've got good message for you. There is a lot more where this came from.

You see, I write thousands of words every month, sent out via my blog create-to-succeed.co.uk and by email to thousands of entrepreneurs, business owners and those who dream of living financially free across the world.

I'm on stage most months, sharing the latest findings from my own business to hundred of other business owners. I run a training programme on Drop Shipping and Fulfilment by Amazon (FBA) helping people to achieve their dream of being financially free.

I know you'll take a whole lot more value from being a member of this programme. All this is available free when you subscribe to my newsletter. Watch the video that I've recorded especially for you at www.create-to-succeed.co.uk

I sincerely hope that you make a right choice. If you've enjoyed my story, and found the lessons in this book to be valuable, I hope that you'll share it with your friend on social media.

But more importantly, I hope you take action on what I share because these methods have transformed my business, my life . . . but only because I implemented them right away. I know that if you take action, even a little bit, that you'll see big changes in your business.

Whatever you decide, I wish you well on your journey for your financial freedom.

To your success,
Jean. T

NOTICE

Our programme does not claim to make you an expert, but rather to help you achieve your dreams and implement your project. With the 20 Golden Secrets of Business Attitude to Succeed, you'll be able to chase away procrastination. This book has nothing to do in get rich quick. We don't believe on shortcut to be rich, only in hard work, adding value and serving others. Our training are intended in the professional manner, to help you find your road and share your message to make a difference in the world, while living a better life and growing your business. By our vision we feel transparency and honesty are important and we hold everyone and ourselves to a high standard of integrity.

By the Law we cannot guarantee, that everyone make any money with this new training or their ability to get results and earn any money with our idea, information, tools or strategies. We don't know you and besides, your results in life are up to you.

We just want to help people by giving great content, direction and strategies that move them forward the same we use in our business. Nothing on this page or any of our websites is a promise or guarantee of results or future earnings, and we do not offer any magic-money-tree solution. Any financial numbers referenced here, or on any of our websites, are simply estimates or projections, and should not be considered exact, actual or as a promise of potential earnings, all numbers are illustrative only.

Thanks for reading this book. Until next time, "Be yourself. Think different. Think big. Treat people with respect and dignity. Follow your dream no matter what. Make it happen and live fully."